AF279316

INSPIRED
BY
Faith

INSPIRED BY

Faith

DEVOTIONS FOR LIVING YOUR GOD-CHOSEN LIFE

EDITORS OF GUIDEPOSTS

A Gift from Guideposts

Thank you for your purchase! We want to express our gratitude for your support with a special gift just for you.

Dive into *Spirit Lifters*, a complimentary e-book that will fortify your faith, offering solace during challenging moments. Its 31 carefully selected scripture verses will soothe and uplift your soul.

Please use the QR code or go to **guideposts.org/ spiritlifters** to download.

Inspired by Faith: Devotions for Living Your God-Chosen Life

Published by Guideposts
100 Reserve Road, Suite E200
Danbury, CT 06810
Guideposts.org

Cover design by Judy Ross
Interior design by Judy Ross
Cover photo by Tatiana Magurova/iStock
Typeset by Aptara, Inc.

ISBN 978-1-961251-59-5 (softcover)
ISBN 978-1-961251-60-1 (epub)

Printed and bound in the United States of America

CONTENTS

The Good Life

Laurie Davies

I once heard a story about a fisherman living the good life in a small coastal village. He rose early, found the best fishing waters, sold his catch, and returned home to play with his kids and take a nap with his wife.

Life was simple, family life sweet.

A businessman met him one morning and said he should catch more fish. With the earnings, he could buy a bigger boat and hire fishermen. Then he could buy a whole fleet. Then he'd be a millionaire.

"But what then?" asked the fisherman.

"Then you could retire, move to a small coastal village, and have time to play with your kids and take naps with your wife," the businessman replied.

The fisherman just smiled. He knew something the businessman didn't know.

He already had that life.

🐚 🐚 🐚

The good life. Winning at life. Living our best life. We hear a lot about these ideas. I must admit that over the years I've had a rolling definition of what they mean. In my twenties, I thought living my best life meant meeting my newspaper deadlines and dating the cute boy I met at church. I also thought it would be nice to own a car with a decent paint job.

In my thirties, I thought winning at life meant winning the Pulitzer Prize or winning mom of the year. Sadly, I didn't win either. But looking back, I learned so much about Jesus in those years. I grew, but in different ways than I had thought I wanted. Week by week and Bible study by Bible study, I began building on a foundation of faith rather than professional achievements or perfectionistic tendencies.

In my forties, "living my best life" became more like "hang on for dear life" as I navigated spine surgeries, relationship losses, and wondering where the aliens took my teenage son's brain matter. I'm happy to report they returned it, and I now have a college graduate who is a ton of fun and wishes his car had a decent paint job.

And in my fifties? The "good life" feels like something different. Something riskier. I've been married to that cute boy from church for 28 years now, and I'm so grateful he is steady because I have a sense that God still has plans ahead that will stretch me. Strangely, it's OK. I'm finally starting to understand that without faith it is impossible to please God.

After all these years, I'm asking God to simply use me how *He* wants to. This has meant hard, humbling work in secret places. Lots of time on my knees. I'm learning to lose my life because Jesus said that's how I would find it. So:

Ego? I don't want it.

My plans? They're never as good as His plans.

Busyness to the point of burnout? Not good and not from God.

Anything coming between God and my relationship with Him? It. Must. Go.

Addition by subtraction. That's my formula for the good life. What's yours? I think it's a question Jesus wants us to explore. After all, He's the one who said: "I have come that they may have life, and have it to the full" (John 10:10, NIV).

The passage hints at something incredible—life lived right to the brim. One so full that the slightest nudge will cause abundance to spill over. This is not a skimping or limping life, one that's barely getting by. It is life that goes past the expected limit. It's maximum life, not minimum life.

How do we find this?

Four words about Jesus give us a clue. "In him was life" (John 1:4, NIV).

Jesus himself offers four more words: "I am … the life" (John 14:6, NIV).

The life we long for is found in Jesus. He gave His life so we could live. Without the burden of rules we couldn't keep. Without the penalty of sin. Without fear.

Faith Paves the Way

Our part in this process is faith.

If we have faith the size of a mustard seed, we can tell mountains to move (Matthew 17:20). That sounds powerful, like a little bit can go a long way. The Bible also says faith is confidence in things we hope for and proof of things we cannot see (Hebrews 11:1). This sounds sturdy, like something we can count on.

Yet, if I'm being totally honest, my faith sometimes resembles a scene I witnessed recently in a jazz club in New York. The Harlem Gospel Choir performed with soaring vocals, but the audience seemed, well…stiff. So, one of the vocalists gave this quick tutorial: "When one of us hits a high note that feels good in your soul, I want somebody to say, 'Won't He do it!' as loud as you can."

Some clapped. Others nodded. One brave soul in the back yelled, "Won't He do it!"

"Let's practice," he said, singing a high note. He thrust a microphone in front of an Italian woman named Alessandra. "Now say, 'Won't He do it!'"

She took a deep breath and worked up her answer.

"WHAT ARE YOU DOING?" she yelled excitedly.

The singer doubled over with laughter, telling the audience we were a tough crowd, but they were going to hit the high notes anyway.

I confess I'm like this. I long to have a *Won't-He-do-it* faith. I believe God has designed a good plan for me. A plan for life to the fullest. But when life gets hard or the assignment feels too big, I blurt out, "What are You doing?"

Keep Moving

As I work out my faith, God is working out "the good life" in me. I wonder sometimes if this is like an assembly line, because I feel like a half-built product. One that's missing a few screws. One who's blown a few gaskets. One who cries out for the Master Craftsman to sand my rough edges or drill His love deep into my soul. I wander. I rush. I hit the emergency stop button and bring the whole operation to a screeching halt.

But He is always making me. Body, mind, and soul. And He's making you too.

Maybe you're at the beginning of your journey and you're not sure how this faith mystery works. You are in for a treat in this volume, as our contributors explore themes that hint at the incredible life God has designed for you. Oh, how I would love to sit with you to hear about the promises you discover in these pages.

Perhaps you started out with Jesus years ago, but red lights of fatigue are flashing or alarms of doubt are blaring. I pray that reflections on God's love remind you why you started and selections on self-care nurture you as you sort things out.

If pain or regret have you staring into the rearview mirror of your life, contributor Cynthia Ruchti's own confrontation with this may inspire you. "I spent so much time rehearsing my past, I had no voice left for discussing my possibilities," she writes on p. 105.

Or maybe you're humming along. Just like the board game Life, you started a career, got married, had kids, and you pointed your car toward retirement. But unlike the board game, some things didn't help you win as you had hoped. Readings on purpose, joy, and relationships may ignite a fresh vision.

Give Yourself Room to Grow

Wherever you are in your faith journey, God delights in making you new. He really does. Consider His promises to us:

❧ "I will give you a new heart, and I will put a new spirit in you. I will take out your stony, stubborn heart and give you a tender, responsive heart" (Ezekiel 36:26, NLT).

❧ "Put on your new nature, and be renewed as you learn to know your Creator and become like him" (Colossians 3:10, NLT).

❧ "For I am about to do something new. See, I have already begun!" (Isaiah 43:19, NLT).

This is a process, and He knows it. Tender, responsive hearts don't learn new rhythms overnight. Becoming like Jesus isn't a magic act where we instantly transform from one thing into another. We can put ourselves in the gentle cycle.

We are new creations *and* God is making us new. We're on the assembly line *and* God sees the finished product. We're desperate to touch the corner of His robe *and* we're more than conquerors. Like the dad in Mark 9 who was frantic to see his son set free from possession by an evil spirit, we declare, *Won't He do it!* ("I believe") and *What are You doing?* ("Help my unbelief").

Life and growth take time. The proof of this is all over the pages of Scripture.

❧ Moses languished in isolation for 40 years before God sent him to set the Israelites free. God didn't use the strong, brash Moses. He wanted a humble, surrendered Moses.

‰ Joseph spent 13 years in slavery and prison. This forged perseverance, leadership, and, ultimately, the ability to see that what others meant for harm, God meant for good (Genesis 50:20).

‰ Peter carried the grief and regret of denying Jesus (Luke 22:62) and became the very rock that Jesus built His church on (Matthew 16:18).

‰ John Mark (the writer of the Gospel of Mark) quit on Paul's first missionary journey and was forbidden by Paul to come on the second (Acts 15:38). Yet Paul, alone and nearing death, specifically wanted John Mark with him at the end (2 Timothy 4:11).

What changed? These people did. God made them physically, mentally, and spiritually strong. He moved them along in His way and in His timing. He helped them grow.

Inspiration and Action

Inspired by Faith invites us into this process by exploring six major themes. Our team of contributing writers has poured out devotions and short reflections on words from Scripture to help you build faith into your life while God builds *you.*

We'll look at *purpose.* Why are we here? I appreciate contributor Brenda L. Yoder's observation on p. 27 that "God's purpose for us isn't always a set point or position." In His hands, our lives are fluid.

We'll explore *love*. This is one of God's favorite topics. Love is why God sent His Son (John 3:16). Because of His great love, we are not consumed (Lamentations 3:22). We love because He showed us how (1 John 4:19).

We'll lean into *personal growth*, the really exciting space where we can trade out old patterns for shiny new ones.

We'll examine *self-care* and what it looks like to work with God to take care of our body, mind, and soul.

We'll discover *joy*—not the kind that hinges on circumstances but as the fruit of a life walked out in faith with God.

And we'll dive into *relationships*, those messy, wonderful human experiments that make us come alive, keep us on our toes, and drive us to our knees.

Inside these pages, you'll find inspiration, action, Scripture, and a whole lot of grace. You'll find practical additions—and subtractions—to help you grow. And the really good news for us is, none of this has to be splashy. In fact, on p. 33 Molly DeFrank reminds us that God sees "meaning in the menial." He places high value on the unheralded work we do. "In the Kingdom of God, the servants are the MVPs…we can please Him with either a microphone or a plunger," she writes.

So, what has God placed in your hands? Is it a microphone or a plunger? A Bible study or a briefcase? A Pulitzer Prize or a diaper bag? He's really interested in seeing it through…with *you*.

Oh, there will be stops and starts. Sometimes you'll feel like a half-built product on an assembly line, tired and not sure you'll make it to the end. You need a loving Maker who will stop the conveyor belt, cup your face in His hands, and say, "But look at how far you've come."

Maybe, like the fisherman, you're already living the good life. And others need the joy you radiate because they badly need a win.

Maybe you want to declare, "Won't He do it!" but you whisper, "What are You doing?" That's OK, you know. God healed the son of a man who said the same thing.

Maybe you've spent too much time rehearsing your past, and God won't let you stay stuck there anymore. You've lost enough. The Author of life has a better story for you.

Whatever your starting point is, we hope that the faith of the contributors to this book inspires *you* to live the good life. Let's dive in together.

It's time.

CHAPTER 1

Purpose

Inspire Hope

As my boys left home, started careers, fell in love, and began families of their own, my role as their mom changed. I chose to see this as a unique season in life that I could use to redefine myself and my purpose. So when I was invited to join a group of women across the US for a 6-week online workshop to discover my two-word purpose statement, I said yes.

The course started with logging in to a website and answering a series of questions. From those answers, I received several words to consider for my two-word purpose statement. As the course went on, participants were encouraged to look up those words in the dictionary to get a full sense of their meaning and whether they resonated with us.

We spent the following 5 weeks asking important questions of one another:

"What has always been true about you?"

"What have been your life-defining moments?"

"What do you want most for others?"

We took turns sharing and discussing these answers. We prayed for one another. And we were challenged to ask those who knew us well what they saw in us and how we positively impacted their lives. I did this and received valuable insights.

At first, I was skeptical that my life purpose could be summed up in two words, but once I chose my purpose statement, I was surprised at how suitable it was for me. What was it? "Inspire Hope."

Hope has been a consistent theme of my life. It's appeared in ways from the serious to the silly. It was a crucial part of my life during the painful period following my alcoholic older brother's suicide. In college, my password to draw funds out of my account was "hope" because I hoped I had cash in there to withdraw. My life verse is Jeremiah 29:11, where God promises to give me hope and a future.

Whether through my writing, my relationships, my conversations with family and friends, or my interactions with the random strangers I meet throughout the day, I long to sow seeds of hope in others. A hopeful life is a meaningful life, a life worth living.

—Jeannie Blackmer

Faith Step: What would your own personal purpose statement be? You can begin the process of finding one by writing your answer to this question: "What do you most want for others?"

Stories and Seashells

Our family recently vacationed in the Pacific Northwest. As our children flew colorful kites and waded through frigid waves, I walked through the wide stretch of beach, enjoying the gritty feeling of sand between my toes. Gulls squawked overhead as I strolled along, noting the various creatures and items washed up on the shore.

I found a beautiful seashell that shimmered with iridescent light. Its surface was like white, polished chalk, but it was broken. Beautiful but shattered. The turbulent waters had battered it beyond repair.

A round stone then caught my attention, worn completely smooth by the pounding waves. The hard edges had been ground away, leaving it pleasant to touch, but the rock was also unremarkable. Dull in color with no interesting features. The surf had beaten it down until it resembled every other stone dotting the shoreline. Lackluster.

As the cold wind tugged my hair across my mouth, I knelt when my toe bumped something altogether different. This rock was not a pretty color, nor did it sparkle, yet it intrigued me the most. Why? Because it bore the imprints of dozens of tiny sea creatures who had once burrowed in its depths and long since had moved on, leaving it full of holes.

It was scarred, but it told me a story. The indelible marks had forever branded it and its journey through the rough ocean waters. It had survived the mighty Pacific to find rest on the shore.

We all have wounds. Some of us put on a show, slapping on our greasepaint and glittering makeup, praying no one will notice how broken we are. Yet the world continues to eat into us until we feel we're only shards of the person God intended us to be. Some of us have let our culture so beat us and mold us that we no longer have our own identity. We look like everybody else and wonder why we feel helplessly lost, unnoticed, and unappreciated. We've thrown away our God-given destiny and are aching to reclaim it.

Some of us are scarred. We may not be polished, glittering, or smooth, but we ought not discount the power of the marks we carry. Scars have the fingerprints of redemption all over them, stories of survival and victory in the hands of the Creator.

Our scars may be the key to unlocking someone else's unique history, and under God's touch, they tell the most amazing stories.

—Tara Johnson

FAITH STEP: What scars do you carry? How could God use them to encourage someone else? ❧

Do not let your adornment be merely outward … rather let it be the hidden person of the heart, with the incorruptible beauty of a gentle and quiet spirit, which is very precious in the sight of God.

—1 Peter 3:3–4 (NKJV)

The usual definition of a "beauty mark" is a molelike mark on the face, but to me a beauty mark is anything that sets a person apart as beautiful. We all have them. Some are obvious: a perfect dimple, long eyelashes, a warm smile, a set of delicate hands. Some are more subtle: "I just love her laugh!" "Her smile lights up the room!"

When we lived in Georgia, we had wonderful neighbors. One woman always knew who was sick and needed a pot of chicken soup. Or who was broken and needed a shoulder to cry on. Her beauty marks were kindness and humility.

Another dear friend was there when you needed help. She cleaned your dishes at the end of a party. Lonely and needing an ear? She showed up. Overwhelmed with packing for a move? She jumped in and wrapped all your china. The beauty marks of service were clear on her.

One precious friend is walking through a difficult diagnosis with grace and dignity. Her faith has been lit on fire despite her deep trials. The kind of faith you apprehend by trusting in nothing but Jesus. Beauty marks of humility.

None of them is famous, but they live and breathe Christ every day. They'd be embarrassed by recognition. They are unconsciously beautiful and are teaching us all how to transfigure drudgery into the divine.

—Kate Battistelli

Tendency to Tinker

I pulled into the driveway and saw that my son Gideon had his head under the hood of his car—again. I groaned. *What's wrong now?* He'd had this car less than 2 weeks, and he'd already spent at least 3 full days working on it. I thought again about the newer, shinier Jeep he'd walked away from at the used car lot. Maybe we should have gotten that one instead. But no. Gideon had found this Jeep, with its lifted frame, oversized tires, torn steering wheel, and missing speakers, and he'd fallen in love. "It has potential," he insisted, and I was outvoted.

"He's working on that car again," I told my husband, Jason, as I walked inside.

"I know," he said with a smile. "It's not even noon yet, and he's awake, outside, and being productive. This is good."

That shifted my perspective. I began to pay more attention to the effect the car was having on my son over the next few weeks. When he wasn't at school or working his part-time job at the grocery store, he was in the driveway tinkering with the Jeep. He seldom slept in. Rarely played video games. Smiled often. Most days, he even had a friend over to help him. What I had seen as a burdensome monstrosity in my driveway, Gideon saw as an enjoyable project to pour himself into.

I thought of the other interests that had captured Gideon's attention over the years—origami, loom bracelets, glass fusing, quilting, 3D printing—and I had a revelation. All of them shared a common thread with his fresh love of auto repair: they all involved working with his hands.

When the time came for Jason and me to help Gideon choose classes for his senior year of high school, we encouraged him to apply for the automotive technology course offered to upper-level students. It's too soon to know if his interest will turn into a career or not, but we knew that the experience would help him lean into his God-given tendency to tinker. The "project car" that I'd seen as a mistake turned out to be the perfect car for him after all.

—Emily E. Ryan

Faith Step: List any activities you view as fun, but others would find burdensome. Add anything that wakes you up early and happy on a Saturday. Ask God what your list reveals.

The Dull, Bland, Unbearable— and Indispensable

I lined up the ingredients for my son's favorite cookies: butter, flour, sugar, baking powder, salt, vanilla, eggs. My five-year-old watched me work, anticipating the treat that would soon dance on his taste buds.

"Mom! Can I taste it?" He pointed to the bowl of dry ingredients: baking powder, flour, and salt. Not a delicious combo.

"You know, Bud, these ingredients aren't delicious on their own. But when you add them to the butter and sugar and eggs, and mix it up just so, it turns into a wonderful treat. It does take a little time, though."

I thought about how odd that might seem to a child who's tasted sweet, delicious cookies before. "If the cookies taste great," his logic might go, "each of the ingredients used to make those cookies would also taste great."

But that's not true at all. Most of the individual ingredients for cookies are terrible on their own. Who has ever thought, "I could really go for a spoonful of flour right about now"? Even the appealing components to cookies are gross on their own. A spoonful of butter? Yuck. Sugar? Too sweet. Alone, I'd never choose them. But together, each ingredient serves an important purpose.

That's when I realized that life is a whole lot like baking.

If I could choose the recipe of my life, I'd never include many of the ingredients that went into it. I'd never choose acne, the tight budget of early marriage, any form of loss or conflict. I'd add a nice helping of carefree vacation days. Oh, and I'd never "crank up the heat": I'd always opt for avoiding family emergencies, tight work deadlines, and difficult relationships altogether.

Come to think of it, my ideal life would be a lot like a bowl of sugar!

Without the real stuff of life—all the ingredients I thought I'd hate—there'd be no treat at the end of the day. Cookies don't reach their final, delicious form until they get a pinch of boring baking powder and several cups of bland flour, along with a hot oven and lots of uncomfortable mixing of all those different elements. On its own, each part of the process seems undesirable. Only the Master Recipe Author knows that each ingredient serves a critical purpose: Awkward phases of our teen years deepen our compassion. Conflict develops understanding. Tight budgets develop restraint. Loss acquaints us with God's comfort.

Like baking cookies, a delicious life requires the bland, sweet, weird, and salty ingredients that a good God made, designed, and prescribed for our lives.

—Molly DeFrank

FAITH STEP: Think of a difficult season in your past. How did you grow as a person as a result of hardship you never thought you wanted? Thank God for redeeming a tough time with growth.

Life and String Beans

I vowed to plant a vegetable garden this year, determined to grow lots of fresh veggies. I had two fabulous raised beds when we lived in New Jersey and a respectable yield during our Florida years. Especially eggplants. And zucchini. You couldn't kill them if you tried. As I planned out my new garden beds, sweet dreams of beets, carrots, lettuce, and beans filled my head.

I had lofty plans and a couple of sunny spots for a decent garden. It would have been perfect—if it hadn't been for the rain gutters.

With shiny packets of heirloom seeds in hand, I dug into the manure and compost and planted the seeds. Green sprouts appeared, and in my zeal, I subscribed to *Organic Gardening* magazine.

Then it began to rain.

Who knew our gutters were stuffed with decades of dead leaves and whatever else the birds had dropped? As water poured off the porch roof, pounding the seeds and baby plants below, my dreams of fresh vegetables morphed into mud. Ruined. Decimated.

Determined to have a successful garden, I planted again, and twice more my garden hopes were dashed, except for two little bean plants. They escaped the watery wrath and continued to climb. Before I knew it, they were entwined around a nearby nandina. Flowers popped out and, lo and behold, beans! Not many but enough to steam one night.

"For we were saved in this hope, but hope that is seen is not hope; for why does one still hope for what he sees? But if we hope for what we do not see, we eagerly wait for it with perseverance" (Romans 8:24–25, NKJV).

I realize how often *I've* been planted and then washed out. And planted and washed out again, my plans turned to mud. But hope is like those little bean plants. It pushes back against the storms raging through our lives, hangs on, and grows.

It produces flowers. And beans. No matter where a vine is put, its nature is to produce fruit. Even straggly plants can produce fruit for now and seeds for later.

No matter what life throws at us or how many times our dreams get washed out, let's trust that the seeds we plant in faith will bear fruit at the proper time. Fruit that may surprise us.

(So, I checked the other day to see if there were any beans and found a bonanza, lots of flowers for more beans. And we cleaned the gutters…)

—*Kate Battistelli*

Faith Step: Have there been times in your life when your hopes were washed out by an unexpected disaster? What can you do to nurture the dreams you have today?

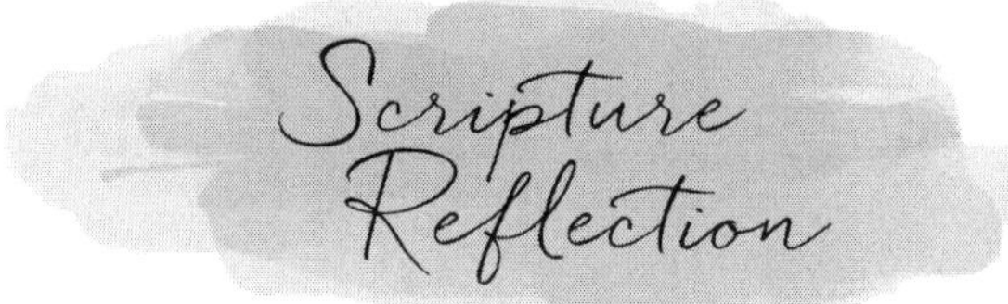

This is the confidence which we have before Him, that, if we ask anything according to His will, He hears us.

—1 John 5:14 (NASB)

"Hi, best mom in the world," my daughter texted while I grocery shopped at Costco. "Remember how you said that you want me to eat more? Well, what would you think of bringing me a cheeseburger at school?"

I laughed aloud in the dairy aisle. What gumption. A different kid, a different day, the answer would've been an easy no.

But after delayed growth and a litany of tests, her doctor recently ordered a high-calorie diet for her. Since then, I've been on a mission to heap on the calories.

"Well, sweet daughter, I don't have time to grab you a cheeseburger. But I'm happy to drop off a slice of Costco pizza at the school."

"Thanks, Mom! You're the best."

I smiled pulling into the school parking lot, surprised by my brief stint as a pizza delivery driver.

All parents know that if your child asks for something that you're able to give her and that aligns with her best interests, you happily consider it. That's why they have the confidence to ask.

And this made me think of our generous Father and how often I underutilize prayer. If I can help fulfill my purpose as a parent by asking for things to help my family, why wouldn't I?

Through Jesus, we have access to God, the most loving and powerful giver. When we pursue His will, we can make our requests with confidence because we know He listens! It's a gift so much better than a slice of pizza.

—Molly DeFrank

Your Life Purpose Isn't One Event

I thought I had life figured out in my twenties and early thirties. Though I had a teaching degree, I found intrinsic purpose as a stay-at-home mom with four young children. I volunteered as a Bible study leader and served in our church, roles that included teaching, working with youth, and mentoring.

I began substitute teaching before my youngest was in school, and later I was unexpectedly offered a full-time teaching position. I was excited to teach history at our local high school and was fully alive in that role for the next several years. My love for history, teaching, and mentoring converged in the classroom. I imagined myself doing that job for many years until I retired.

Then life got complicated. As a full-time working mom with kids from early elementary to high school, I was pulled in various directions. I drove the kids to three different schools before arriving at my own to teach 180 teens. The task of grading assignments for that many students accompanied me to my children's after-school sporting events and into the late-night hours after everyone else was in bed.

Though I loved teaching, the workload wasn't sustainable. I needed more stress-free moments with my children before they grew up and left home. At 40, I decided to leave the classroom and obtain dual master's degrees in clinical mental health counseling and school counseling, which I hoped would provide more flexible work opportunities as my family life changed.

On my last day of teaching school, as I packed up my classroom and turned out the lights, I felt defeated. Teaching had been my passion. Even though I had decided on my new course, I wasn't enthusiastic about it. I couldn't see how another role could be as rewarding.

However, the career change turned out to be even more beneficial than I'd hoped. It allowed me the flexibility to focus on my family as my children grew and also led me to new career opportunities I wouldn't have considered otherwise. Today, I work full-time doing several things I love, including a part-time position as an elementary school counselor, doing other work in private practice, writing, and speaking.

My experience has taught me that God's purpose for us isn't always a set point or position. Instead, it's a lifelong journey of prayerfully discerning when we're not making the time for the important things in life—and then trust that God will guide us to the best place for our present and future needs.

—*Brenda L. Yoder*

Faith Step: Consider your current commitments in this moment of your life, and pray for God's guidance on which fit with His purposeful intent for your life and which do not. Trust that He will guide you to where you're supposed to be, even if you don't understand why.

Shiny Things

I did not know that mice like jewelry until I gave my piano to a friend from church. When the tuner showed up at her house, he suggested she might want to vacuum deep inside. It's not that unusual to find a mouse nest in a piano, apparently. Sure enough, my old piano had one, and my friend said they found three of my earrings in the nest.

And here I'd thought I was just very good at misplacing jewelry.

Fancy critters! Were the mice simply attracted by shiny things? Intent on making a little cash through online second-hand sales? I can't imagine the cost of their rodent dental work after biting into a piece of pretend silver.

The lure of shiny things is not a new trend. Fishermen have capitalized on the principle for years. Throw something shiny in the water—shiny with a hook—and watch what bites. Fish can't resist. And neither can we humans.

"Make five figures a month with no effort on your part" is the latest version of the shiny attraction. "You can earn real dollars playing Solitaire online so you can quit your job."

When did God ever say, "Pursue gold and silver. Accumulate as much as you can. The goal is to set a standard for how high an income you can make while doing the least amount of work possible"? Never. He has a lot to say, though, about not investing in material things that can rust or fade. There is quite a bit of His counsel about working hard and dedicating our efforts to Him, about avoiding the lure of fortune and valuing sacrifice instead.

One of the most poignant moments in Scripture, in my opinion, is when King David longed to thank God for a recent victory and a farmer offered the king everything he'd need—wood for the fire, an animal to sacrifice, the venue. David responded, "I will not sacrifice to the LORD my God burnt offerings that cost me nothing" (2 Samuel 24:24, NIV).

How different from the attitude "I desire all the things and hope they cost me nothing." *Lord, may I find purpose today not in what I can accumulate or the work I can avoid, but in the effort I can offer You. And may I pursue that which shines the spotlight on You.*

—*Cynthia Ruchti*

FAITH STEP: Consider carefully where you may put too much value on what has no more meaning than earrings on a mouse. ✎

The Ministry of Presence

As I neared the age of 60, I desired to slow down and spend more time with the people I care about. We had also recently lost our house in a wildfire, and rebuilding required my time and attention. So, I decided it was a logical time to step down from a position on staff at a worldwide ministry for moms and limit myself to writing for special projects if needed. That way I could focus my attention on the rebuild and have more flexibility in my schedule to choose how I wanted to spend my days and with whom I wanted to spend more time.

At first, I was relieved when I didn't have to battle traffic when driving an hour each way into the office or to attend required staff meetings. But as I selected bathtubs, decided on paint colors, and looked at endless light fixtures, I felt purposeless. These decisions seemed insignificant compared to the job I'd left, where I could focus energy on loving and encouraging moms. *Am I doing anything noteworthy for the world?* I wondered. I didn't have upcoming conferences, workshops, or urgent meetings. I didn't have an inbox full of emails that I needed to answer. My most important decision of the day was how high do I want the toilet paper roll on the wall. Honestly, I missed feeling important.

As I grappled with my conflicting emotions over my career transition, I read a quote from Henri Nouwen: "It is a privilege to have the time and the freedom to practice this simple ministry of presence." This quote shifted my thinking. I had the opportunity to simply be with people, to give them my attention and perhaps lift them up in ways that I couldn't have when I was busy with my old job. Now I had the freedom to do so, and it *was* a privilege. I scheduled long hikes, reconnected with friends I hadn't seen in a while, enjoyed conversations, and said yes to spontaneous invitations.

And what a privilege I had to rebuild our home and thoughtfully create a special space to invite others into. A place to continue this ministry of presence. I discovered new reassurance that my life does have eternal significance. I'm letting go of the need to keep busy and replacing it with enjoying the freedom and privilege to be present with others—not so I feel important but so that others feel loved.

—*Jeannie Blackmer*

FAITH STEP: Invite someone into your home today for coffee or tea and enjoy some leisurely time together.

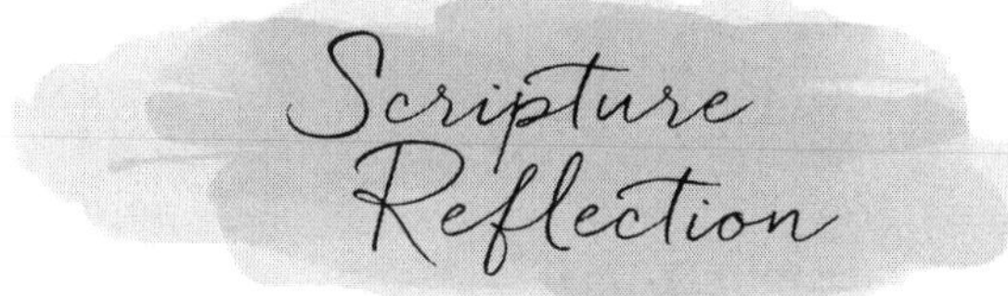

Therefore we also have as our ambition, whether at home or absent, to be pleasing to Him.

—2 Corinthians 5:9 (NASB)

I'd prayed for this professional opportunity for more than a year and was thrilled when God said yes. I hopped on an airplane and landed at my destination, where I shared my message with an audience that was grateful to hear it. For a long, lovely day, I enjoyed a sense of accomplishment and satisfaction. I flew home that night, grateful and excited to hug my husband and kids.

After goodnights, I exhaustedly slumped into bed. This day could not have gone better.

Then I heard it.

"Mooom? I don't feel good," my son called to me from the bathroom.

My eyes flicked open. I hurried to find my boy standing in front of the toilet, about to be sick. Only problem? The toilet was, um, jammed. If I didn't unclog this mess within 5 seconds, I'd need a hazmat suit for what came next. A surge of adrenaline hit me. I plunged like my life depended on it. Crisis averted.

After helping my little sickie get comfortable, I collapsed back into bed. I laughed at the juxtaposition between how my day began and how it ended.

A beautiful thing happens when we anchor our ambitions in pleasing the Lord. We discover meaning in the menial. In the Kingdom of God, the servants are the MVPs. The world might not value small, ugly tasks. But God does. What encouragement knowing that we can please Him with either a microphone or a plunger.

—Molly DeFrank

Upcycled Beauty

A friend recently found an outdated, unabridged *Webster's* dictionary buried in her closet and asked if I wanted it. I had no idea what I'd do with the 60-year-old hardback, but even with its antiquated entries and too-tiny print, I still sensed it had more to give. A few weeks later, when my principal unveiled a new enrichment program that would allow teachers to offer 4-day minicourses on any idea or activity we were passionate about, I knew it was the perfect opportunity to breathe life back into the old dictionary.

Over the next several weeks, I taught almost forty students how to transform the dilapidated pages of an unwanted book into original, whimsical Christmas decor. First, they used craft scissors to cut out hundreds of concentric circles ranging from 1 to 6 inches in diameter. Then I gave each student a wooden base with a small dowel inserted into the center. Starting with the largest circles, they crumpled each page tightly in their hands before flattening it out again and carefully feeding it onto the dowel. After dozens of layers had been added, I glued a green pom-pom to the top of each one and smiled as the students admired their new creations—cute little Christmas trees crafted from the pages of an old book.

The students were proud of their handiwork, but for me, the real joy came in watching what they did after their trees were finished. Some continued decorating with ribbons or glitter, allowing their artistic abilities to shine. Others displayed impressive ingenuity by creating original decorations from the discarded scraps of paper. A few exhibited kindness and generosity as they gave their trees away as gifts. One entrepreneurial girl returned from the break and shared that she had sold her tree for $20.

I was amazed and inspired by how much joy and beauty had come from the insides of a discarded, rejected dictionary, and it reminded me how much hidden potential can come to light when things—and people—are given new opportunities. If we could create so much from so little, I could only imagine how God could still use me.

—Emily E. Ryan

Faith Step: Choose one item in your home to repurpose or upcycle. As you work, ask God to reveal your own hidden potential.

Hopes and Dreams

I spent this morning reworking a children's book where the text is written in a poetic meter similar to that of Dr. Seuss. Finding the perfect rhythm with just the right emphasis on the third beat can be tricky. But I love it.

My unusual task is the result of a partnership to author a series of children's books for a nonprofit whose mission is to promote generosity. Writing these books has been a dream come true. Coming up with nonsense words? Creating funny rhymes? Shaping adorable characters? *How can it get any better than that?*

As a college student, I had harbored secret dreams of being a children's author. My first story was a simple fairy tale inspired by the birth of my first-ever niece, Alyson. I felt certain it would be published within months. It still sits in my writing folder, waiting for its moment.

As a young pastor's wife and mom of three boys, I leaned heavily into the knowledge that while my writing needed to take a back seat so that I could focus on family, writing was in my future. Even when months would pass by when my keyboard remained untouched, I kept notes on my phone with the beginnings of stories. I filled journals with doodled characters. Dozens of picture books have been sorted into different folders on my computer. These are the hopes and dreams that are yet to be fulfilled.

But this morning, as I sit in front of my screen, sipping my coffee and leaning into my inner poet, I recognize that my purpose goes way beyond my dreams of crafting stories. It also encompasses more than being a wife or a mother to some very active boys. It has taken me years to finally realize that my true path and purpose is to love God and glorify Him with whatever I am doing.

My hopes and dreams are exceeded when I place them into the hands of the One who loves me most of all. When I find my purpose in loving Him, He weaves His goodness through every season and every task. He shapes my character with His deep truth. He determines the rhythm and meter of my days with His mercy and grace. *How can it get any better than that?*
—*Susanna Foth Aughtmon*

FAITH STEP: What hopes and dreams do you have at this moment? Take a moment to pray, placing them in the hands of the One who loves you most of all, and ask Him to use them for His purpose.

A Place to Belong

I've always felt slightly out of place in our fast-paced modern culture. Even when I was young, I was more comfortable reading about history or learning from older folks than trying the newest makeup trends or buying popular gadgets. I've often believed I'd be better suited to living in a different time period, or that living away from a society's pressures would usher in a feeling of belonging. I've often assumed true contentment and happiness were out of reach because I didn't have what it took to succeed in a hustle-ridden culture where it seemed as though you must constantly strive at home and work to be satisfied.

Then came the pandemic. The fast pace of life around me slowed down—the cultural pressure to strive and achieve that had made me feel trapped now dissipated as everyone was forced to stop and reassess.

One day, while sitting on our front-porch rocker during the lockdown, I realized I had something to offer the modern world. Many people were rediscovering old-fashioned values and processes, like making sourdough bread from scratch or learning to knit. Guests who came for a staycation in our Airbnb suite during the months-long travel restrictions said they appreciated the older books, antiques, and quilts that made them feel at peace when visiting our home. I felt more comfortable offering sage perspectives from older, more thoughtful times to counseling clients and online followers as these ideas gained new popularity. I felt at home in my life in a brand-new way as others began to value what had felt out of place before.

I had always wondered if God had made a mistake by creating me as I was in this life He designed for me. Now I began to ask myself if my unique skills and mindset were actually well matched for the culture around me. It was a thought I hadn't considered before.

As the months of the ongoing pandemic unfolded, for the first time I accepted that there wasn't something wrong with me—that, in fact, I had the skills and perspectives others needed now. God showed me that dreaming about what I could do in another place and time was a useless waste of energy. I understood, in a way I never could have otherwise, that God created me—and you—with a unique, satisfying purpose for our lives right now.

—*Brenda L. Yoder*

Faith Step: Do you ever feel as if you'd be better suited for a different kind of life? Ask God to show you how you're perfectly suited for the current life He created for you. Write down all the ways you contribute to this world as daily affirmations you can see, recite, or pray.

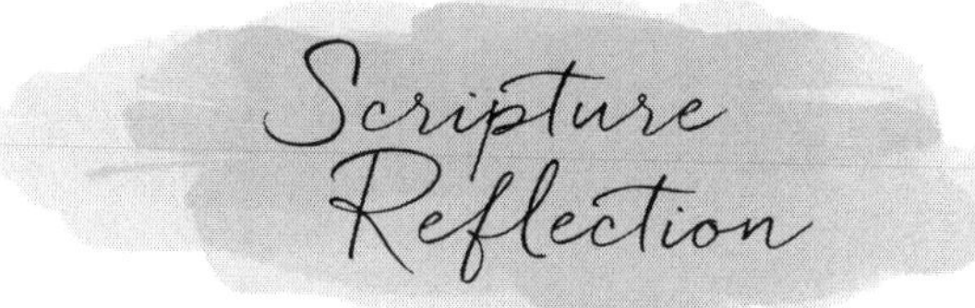

Then he said to him, "Rise and go; your faith has made you well."

—Luke 17:19 (NIV)

Imagine you and your best friend sipping tea and letting your thoughts and conversation turn philosophical.

"Do you have life goals? What are they?"

After some thought, your friend answers, "I want to live a so-so life."

"So-so? What kind of goal is that?"

Your friend seems confused. Then she says, "What? No. You misunderstood me. I want to live a *sozo* life. Big difference."

The Greek word *sozo* encompasses a wide range of meanings, including *helped, healed, delivered,* and *saved,* as well as one that caught me up short—*made whole.*

One of the many appearances of the word *sozo* in Scripture is this one recorded in Luke 17. Jesus healed ten men of leprosy, a horrid, devastating disease. Set free from all that had handicapped and complicated their lives, that had kept them sequestered as unclean and outcasts, nine of them went on their merry way. One—only one—returned to thank Jesus, enthusiastically.

Jesus marveled that none of the others had thought to return to thank God for the gift they'd been given. Only the one. Jesus said to the man, "Rise and go; your faith has made you well." The King James Version translates the word *well* here as *whole (sozo).*

Whole—in body, mind, and spirit. Healed and delivered and saved and helped on every level. And when brought full circle, as it was with the single, humbled no-longer-a-leper? Grateful.

Who wouldn't want to live a *sozo* life?

—*Cynthia Ruchti*

Pursue Life with Others

We were made for people. God did not create us to live life alone, but to participate in life with others. But at times of transition, such as a move or the loss of someone you love—especially given our increased reliance on technology for almost everything—many of us drift into isolation and loneliness. In fact, the US surgeon general declared loneliness an epidemic. Scientific research has shown it to be even more devastating to your health than smoking fifteen cigarettes a day. He also emphasized that about one in two adults in America experiences loneliness.

I've recently experienced a season of loneliness. My husband, Zane, and I rented a house in a neighborhood we used to live in while our home was under construction. I imagined it would be like the days when we previously lived there, with neighbors constantly getting together. Instead, like me, many of the neighbors we had previously known had moved away. Those still nearby were busy with work, travel, living part-time in another state, or enjoying time with grandkids. Most were not as available to spend time with me as I had imagined.

My loneliness came from other factors too. I have a close group of girlfriends whom I've prayed with for 20 years. We met at a church in our community when our children were young. Many of those women, too, have relocated, so our in-person times are rare. We do still pray on Zoom once a month, and for that I am grateful. Technology does offer some unique ways of being with others, but nothing replaces face-to-face.

While it's not easy to make new friends, I believe that maintaining old friendships and seeking out new ones should be a lifelong pursuit. That means committing to actively pursuing friendships and inviting others into your life. To combat my loneliness, I decided to start a game night with couples who could walk over to our house, and that opened the door to new friendships.

If you're in a season of loneliness, know you're not alone. But don't wait for others to invite you into their lives—you can be the one to make that happen. Be purposeful in pursuing friendships, and your loneliness will eventually lessen.

—*Jeannie Blackmer*

FAITH STEP: Invite a neighbor over today to make cookies with you or enjoy a cup of tea and chat.

Reputation for Faithfulness

A young person I care about is in an awkward position. He needs a job. He's bright and has energy to spare. What he lacks is faithfulness.

He's a master at excuse-making but has not yet found a paying position matching that skill set. In the part-time, minimum-wage jobs he's held—temporarily—it's been a struggle for him to show up every day. He's "sick." Or tired. Or didn't know the schedule had been changed. Or forgot to look at the schedule for the new week. Or forgot it was a new week.

So he has no references or positive recommendations when he searches for a new job. He has not built a reputation for faithfulness. Sweet and lovable isn't enough in the work world.

He's not alone, of course. His experience—hard as it is for him—is ripe with lessons for me. The main purpose of a job when you're just starting out is not the money that goes in your pocket. It's building a reputation for faithfulness, one that can extend to every area of our lives.

Psalm 33:4 tells us that God is "faithful in all he does" (NIV). I imagine He would lead the way in returning grocery carts to the cart rack; replacing an unwanted frozen item in the freezer section, not on the bread shelf; providing for us even when we've been wasteful or unwise.

We can show our faithfulness to Him through our own actions. I believe that God is less concerned about how long I spend in His Word than He is with my faithfulness to *come* to His Word. That He doesn't count the number of sentences or minutes in my last prayer—He's grateful I *turned* to Him. That He cares less about how successful my latest endeavor turned out than He is with the fact that I showed up both when things were going well and when they weren't, when I felt like it and when I didn't.

God is moved by our faithfulness. It's nonnegotiable for living a rewarding, fulfilling, meaningful life as a God follower.

I count on His faithfulness. Can He count on mine?

—*Cynthia Ruchti*

FAITH STEP: Take a moment to reflect on the ways or times you've been faithful to God and to those He's entrusted to you, even when it hasn't been easy. Remind your soul that your faithfulness registers with God—and you're building a commendable reputation for it.

*So then faith comes by hearing,
and hearing by the word of God.*

—Romans 10:17 (NKJV)

I must admit, sometimes God makes me laugh out loud. He uses the most mundane things to get my attention. Does He do that with you too?

I'd flipped on my GPS (maybe one of the world's greatest techno gadgets) for directions to my friend's house. In flipping it on, somehow, I switched it to the nighttime setting. It was a sunny morning, and its screen nearly blacked out the roads it was leading me to.

I was utterly frustrated, even though I could still hear the directions. Ours has a lilting British female voice. (We call her Fiona.) But I couldn't see where I was going.

I kept poking the screen as I drove, thinking that by poking it, I could magically force it to change. Nope. Not happening. "Come on, Lord, help me; I can't see where I'm going!" Then it hit me. Loud and clear. "Faith comes by hearing." I knew God was putting His emphasis on that moment to drive it deep into my spirit.

When we can't see the road in front of us, let's listen to His voice for guidance. He speaks in the darkness, and we *will* hear if we have ears to hear. I chuckle because He knows me so well. I don't hear a rumbling voice from heaven. No. He gets my attention *with a gadget.*

I'm planning to use my slow cooker today. Wonder what's on His lesson plan?

—Kate Battistelli

CHAPTER 2

Love

Extravagant Love

When my daughter was born, I had no clue what to expect. I knew absolutely nothing about babies. When I was holding her that first time and gazing at her little face as she nursed or slept, waves of love flooded my heart. I'd never experienced anything that could compare to this kind of love. I swore to love her forever, guarding her life with mine, as I counted tiny fingers and toes, reveled in warm snuggles, heard her soft breath as she rested on my chest and felt my heartbeat…the regular rhythm she'd heard as she grew in the womb. I couldn't imagine such a fierce love could drench my heart. A love I would always protect. I would do all in my power to raise her as the woman of God that He had called her to be, helping her find her purpose and destiny. That pure devotion and warmth between us created a mother-and-child bond that's anchored us for life.

As I watched my daughter grow, I marveled at the incredible gift God had given me. *Me.* The one who had refused to acknowledge my deep need for Him until I was 29 and had lived decades denying Him. Oh, the wonder of His love for us! It was that experience of holding my daughter that taught me not only the depth of God's love but also what an extraordinary, precious gift He offers—the capacity to feel that love ourselves.

God *is* love. We've heard it so often it's lost its power, but we can express His love in the subtlest of ways. The smile and helping hand to the mom at the grocery store struggling to wrangle her kids and her groceries into the car. Visiting a loved one at the nursing home. Flowers and a note left on a grieving widow's front porch. A hot meal to the family that just moved in down the street.

All of our small acts of kindness display the extravagant love of the Father. Extraordinary acts of service from ordinary folks that drive back the darkness.

He does the same for us.

—Kate Battistelli

FAITH STEP: Visualize a person whom you love unconditionally, deeply, and fiercely. Take a moment to feel that emotion deep inside you. Now imagine God pouring that kind of love onto you.

My Dating Experience

Experts say couples should keep dating no matter how long they've been married. For years, my husband and I have called Wednesday evening our "date night" because both of us enjoy watching the same TV show that night. Sometimes we even make popcorn.

You might say that love isn't made of dates. But today it was.

After my 3-day work trip, my husband and I reconnected. We talked for a few minutes before I stopped mid-sentence because of what lay on the counter.

"Honey, what did you do? Did you…? Are those…?"

"I saw them when I was at the store and thought of you."

"Medjool dates? My favorite!"

"I know."

A green plastic container of pitted Medjool dates was his way of saying "I love you." And the message got through loud and clear. If you arrange them just right, you *can* spell LOVE with dates.

Would I have also appreciated a nice steak dinner and a dozen red roses? Sure. But what I'll remember long into the future are those sweet dates he left for me on the counter.

I don't want to miss the lesson inside that green plastic container. If I'm waiting for a major prayer to be answered and fail to notice God's love gift of a safe trip home in a blinding snowstorm…If I open myself to God's love during a worship service but don't pick up on the wonder of His love gift of an unexpected blessing…If I can see His love when enraptured

by a cherished truth in His Word but not in a timely note
from a friend…

How do I *know* God loves me? We said so in our "vows"
long ago. He promised it to me in His Word and with the
gift of His Son. And I told Him of my love when I acknowl-
edged Him as my Savior and my Lord. We do have more
formal "date nights" when the candles are burning and our
attention is solely focused on each other (or rather, mine
is solely focused on Him, since He's *always* attentive). But,
like Medjool dates on the counter, life is scattered with
unremarkable, sweet reminders that He cares.

—Cynthia Ruchti

Faith Step: Express your love for someone in an unexpected
but thoughtful way today. And make sure you notice how God's
love shows up around you today too.

Love Is a Choice

S ave that couch in the corner and pull up some extra chairs," I told my sister. "I'll go find everyone else." I ran into my younger brother and his wife in the church foyer and told them we were meeting in the café. When I found our parents in their Sunday school class, they didn't hesitate to join us either. "We're just struggling to understand," I told them as we walked, and they nodded and quickened their steps.

Soon, all eight of us—my younger siblings and I, our spouses, and our parents—were seated knees to knees in the church café, speaking in hushed voices as we tried to untangle the news we'd received over the weekend. Our oldest brother and his wife had announced their divorce after more than 20 years of marriage. The rest of us were left reeling with confusion, sadness, and questions. Did we miss signs of trouble? Could we have done anything differently to support them? What happens now?

Several times as we talked, friends from church noticed our intimate family huddle and waved or stopped by to chat. No one knew that our gathering was more of an emergency family meeting than a casual Sunday morning coffee date. No one knew that we were collectively hurting, mourning the loss of the family unit we had known for more than 20 years. No one knew we were conflicted inside, struggling with how to best show love in this new, unfamiliar season of brokenness. Instead, they commented on what they saw on the surface.

"Aren't y'all the cutest?" one said as she passed by. "Your family is so blessed," said another. "It must be nice to have such a beautiful, close family."

We responded with our best beauty-pageant smiles, but I realized that even if the observations were incomplete, the comments still rang true. Our family was indeed blessed, but not because we were perfect and polished or able to coordinate outfits for a family portrait. We were blessed because in every season, the good and the bad, we responded in the same way. We turned to each other, drew strength from the Lord, and chose to love each other through it. This season, as hard as it was, would be no different.

—Emily E. Ryan

Faith Step: Love is, first and foremost, a choice. Think of the person or people in your life who are in a challenging situation. Are you having trouble figuring out how best to support them? Choose to simply love them, even if you're not sure how. Even better, ask the Lord to love them through you. ✤

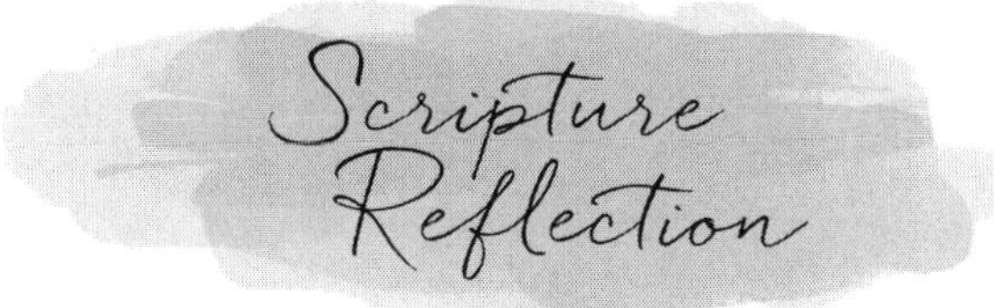

*Oh give thanks to the L*ORD*,
for he is good, for his steadfast
love endures forever!*

—PSALM 107:1 (ESV)

Psalm 107 is filled with mini stories wrapped in one big story that emphasizes the steadfast love of the Lord. One of the mini stories is about sailors suffering due to the power of the ocean waves. They became so seasick they staggered as if drunk. They were at their wits' end until the Lord had mercy and calmed the waves (Psalm 107:23–31).

Our family recently experienced a fraction of the power of the ocean and our lack of control over it while scuba diving. In the middle of a dive, the currents suddenly changed. Underwater surges started to lift us up 20 feet, then drop us 20 feet. We had absolutely no control. It was scary. Our dive guide motioned us to follow him, and we swam to the boat.

Once safely on board, we traveled back to land on choppy water. A few people got seasick. Our boat captain said he's seen people get so seasick that they curl up in the fetal position under the boat benches and "lose their minds."

We can feel crazy when life's waves knock us for a loop. And feeling out of control is scary—sometimes it can even make us physically sick. Thankfully, we have a God who is in complete control, and He reassures us with his steadfast love. Sometimes circumstances change when we pray for an end to the storm and sometimes they don't, but God's unwavering love keeps the waves from overwhelming us.

—Jeannie Blackmer

What a Pedicure Taught Me about Washing Feet

I got a pedicure this week. I checked in, picked my polish, and, with iPhone in hand, relaxed in the big massage chair, eagerly awaiting the warm, soothing water, the solitude, and the leg massage.

Typically, a kind employee fills the foot bath while I check Instagram, remaining disconnected and disinterested in the human being *washing my feet.*

I felt the Lord prompting me to talk to her and ask her name. So, I did. I learned her name was Kim and she's from Vietnam.

As we chatted, she explained that she's been here 10 years and has two children, a girl and a boy. She got married in Vietnam and was able to come to America because her husband was in the military.

I asked if she ever got back home. She replied that her family can't visit here, so she must go there, but she only goes when she can afford to.

As we chatted, it struck me how easily I let strangers who cross my path remain invisible and anonymous. Service people. The checkout girl. The college kid making my chai latte. The waitress. Or this precious lady studiously scrubbing my feet and polishing my toes.

Sitting there, I recalled how Jesus served without fanfare. As she applied the polish, He gently whispered, "She has worth too." *She is not anonymous.*

We ignore so many who cross our paths. I don't want to ignore anymore. I want to make an extra effort and be willing to smile, talk, and shine love on the ones I'm prone to overlook, finding ways to love like *He* loved.

I decided to get to know Kim. Next month, I'll request her and let her upsell me the extra-special aromatherapy pedicure. I'll tip her well, putting my money where my mouth is—or, in this case, where my feet are.

What if we all connected with someone we don't usually notice, giving without asking anything in return by laying down our agendas and showing Christ's love? Wash *their* feet. We don't have to be heroes; we only have to *notice*.

One pebble dropped in the middle of the ocean can become a tidal wave when it reaches shore. And one intentional act of love can change the world.

—Kate Battistelli

Faith Step: Is there someone you come across on a regular basis that you don't pay attention to? Or maybe someone you've never met who could use some extra love from you? Take the time to notice them today.

Love Is Sticky

I've pondered the best way to describe love for years, and the best adjective I can manage is *sticky*. It won't let go. It clings. No matter the condition, love stays, refusing to give up. It extends forgiveness and blessings over and over again.

My son and I often play a little game called "Would You Love Me Even Then?" One of us asks the other if we would still love each other if crazy things altered our appearance, personality, or situation. Nate asks me questions like, "Mom, what if my hair was made out of spaghetti? Would you love me even then?" "What if my toes were made of hot dogs? Would you love me even then?" I assure him my love will never change, spaghetti hair or hot dog toes notwithstanding.

I've asked him, "Nate, what about when Mommy is really old? Will you love me even then?" He always pats my cheek and smiles. "I'll always love you, Mommy!"

"What about days when I'm cranky? Do you love me even then?"

Nate giggles. "Everyone is cranky sometimes. Of course I'll love you."

One day, Nate climbed into my lap and sighed. "Hey, Mom?"

"Yes, Buddy?"

"What if I did something really bad? Would you love me even then?"

I smiled and kissed the top of his head, squeezing him close. "Sweetie, it doesn't matter how much you mess up. Nothing will ever, ever keep me from loving you."

Love never fails. And as love perseveres, grace continues to pour out blessings and gifts on the recipient, whether deserved or not.

Love is forgiveness, no matter the wrong. Love is giving a gift with no strings attached and no need for a thank-you. Love is taking a meal to someone who has hurt your feelings. Love is the Son of God hanging from a cross to redeem a world of hopeless prisoners.

There is nothing stickier than a love that refuses to let go.

—*Tara Johnson*

FAITH STEP: Make a list of ways you can show "sticky love" to people in your world (teachers, mail carriers, garbage collectors, neighbors, cranky acquaintances) and then create a plan to bring your ideas to fruition.

Grace That Covers More than What We See

My dad handed me an envelope with my name on it. "Open it when you get back to your dorm room." He closed his car door and gave me a hug.

"Enjoy your flight, Dad." As he walked away, I opened the envelope. A card of encouragement—and a generous stack of cash.

A few hours later, I called him.

"Hey, Dad. Just making sure you got home OK."

"Sure did. Hey, did you open the card?" he asked.

Dad and I had a close relationship. One that included plenty of joking. That, and the fact that I was a 19-year-old knucklehead, made me respond like this:

"No, I didn't get to open it. The windows were open on the drive home, and the envelope flew out on the freeway. Hope nothing special was inside." I smiled, waiting for him to flip out.

But he didn't. Not even a second passed before he replied.

"Nope, just a card telling you how proud I am of you."

My mouth dropped. *What?* He had half a second to process that I had just cost him a few hundred bucks—poof, out the window. But it was more important that his daughter not feel guilty about losing it.

I quickly told him I was kidding, and I thanked him for the gift. We laughed about my bad joke. But I'll never forget that glimpse into my father's heart.

I've thought of this story over the years, how the love of my earthly father reflected the kindness and care of my heavenly one.

God, the inventor of love and grace, has made and moved oceans for His children. He has sacrificed for us in ways that are impossible to quantify. We can grasp much of His love through His Word.

The more we ponder it, the more we catch glimpses of His love enveloping us, covering us, lavishing grace on us—even from the day we were born.

—Molly DeFrank

FAITH STEP: Stop to ponder the innumerable ways God has shown grace or covered you in love. Remember that even before you were born, Jesus died for you. Praise God for His generous love.

The Lord *your God is with you,*
the Mighty Warrior who saves.
He will take great delight in you;
in his love he will no longer
rebuke you, but will rejoice
over you with singing.

—Zephaniah 3:17 (NIV)

From the moment the doctor laid my baby girl in my arms, my heart melted. I'll never forget when Bethany looked up at me with her big blue eyes and studied my face. I was so overcome with joy, I sang "Jesus Loves Me" over and over in that white, sterile delivery room. And I've been singing over her ever since.

When she was six years old, she happily found me in the kitchen, wrapped her chubby fingers around mine, and tugged me into her bedroom. She couldn't wait to show me how she had made her bed all by herself. The covers were rumpled and the pillow was cockeyed, but I smiled and praised her for her accomplishment. Would the bed ever grace the cover of a design magazine? No, but it was beautiful in my eyes because of the joy the effort had brought her.

As she grew, it didn't matter if she brought me mangled wildflowers, a stick-figure drawing, or crayon-scrawled letters on wrinkled paper; I delighted in her. She's 21 now and nothing has changed. I adore everything about my daughter and the woman she has become.

As strong as a mother's love is for her child, God's love for each of us is infinitely greater. We are like eager children, running to show Him our best efforts—our accomplishments and accolades. Surely to Him, they must look like rumpled bedding. Yet He smiles. He laughs. He praises.

He delights in us.

—Tara Johnson

Twenty Reasons to Love

We were days away from our twentieth wedding anniversary, and my husband, Jason, and I were having a standoff in our bathroom. Since both of us were tired from a series of unexpected minor emergencies on top of the unusually high demands of December, our tempers were short and our patience was limited. I, especially, was on the verge of a meltdown.

"I have an idea," Jason said when it was clear we weren't making any progress. "For our anniversary, let's each make a list of twenty things we love about each other."

I flared my nostrils. "Can we also make a list of twenty grievances?" I asked, not sure if I was joking or not.

He laughed. "No grievances allowed. It might be hard, but I think it will be good."

On the night of our anniversary, as we sat beside each other at our favorite restaurant, a fancy steak place, we shared our lists. We'd long since made up from our pre-Christmas squabble, so we were able to enjoy the moment for all it was worth. As it turns out, we agreed, making the lists was easier than we thought. Once we started brainstorming, we both had to make ourselves stop at only twenty items. Had we wanted, we could have easily added more.

We also noticed that many items on our lists were similar. We both love that the other has a strong faith, places a high value on family, has a keen sense of humor, and continues to invest in personal growth. I love that he is a hands-on dad. He loves that I am a devoted mom. We both agreed that our lives are richer because the other is in it.

The most surprising discovery was that our lists gave us insight into our challenges as well. As we talked through our observations, we saw that sometimes the things we love most about each other are also the things that frustrate us the most. He loves that I am independent, but my stubborn insistence on doing things for myself can aggravate him at times. I love that he can seamlessly manage so much of our lives, but occasionally his efficiency feels controlling rather than helpful. Seeing this, and talking through the best and worst parts of who we are as a couple, helped us solidify what we already knew in our hearts: we are both in it for another 20 years together.

—Emily E. Ryan

Faith Step: Make a list of twenty things you love about your spouse or a child, parent, or friend. Be vulnerable enough to share it—and to hear what they say in return. ☙

My First Love

We had a visiting guest speaker in church yesterday. He encouraged us to return to our first love, asking us to remember the first moment we were overwhelmed by God's incredible love.

I flashed back to my early twenties. I had been in a rough place. I was overcoming an eating disorder and had almost flunked my junior year of Bible college. I didn't know how to reconcile my mistakes and struggles with what I knew of God. He was holy, all-powerful, and all-knowing—and I was a mess. I wasn't sure how He felt about me.

I decided to take a gap year and attend discipleship school. Each day we sat in on lectures, sharing about God's goodness and grace. But I felt broken and vulnerable.

Until, one morning, a guest speaker described a word picture based on a phrase in Zephaniah 3:17 (NIV): "He will take great delight in you; in his love he will no longer rebuke you, but will rejoice over you with singing." The speaker said the phrase *rejoice over you with singing* meant *to lift and spin around*, like a daddy scooping up his child, whooping with laughter. He had us imagine being a small child lifted and held with great delight.

I began to cry. The thought of my Heavenly Father grabbing me up in a fun-filled embrace changed everything. God wasn't rebuking me, even with all my problems and mistakes. In His great love, He was holding me close. He was crazy about me!

I was forgiven. Loved. Celebrated! At that moment, I began to fall in love with the One who loves me most of all! He cares for me—body, mind, and spirit.

Yesterday, sitting in a pew 30 years and thousands of miles from the place where I first felt God's love for me, I was overwhelmed once again. Tears slipped down my face. It's funny how that happens when I sense God's love. He sees my mistakes. He forgives me and calls me back to that place of deep love and wild joy one more time! My best life begins when I remember who God is. He is my Heavenly Father. He cares for me—body, mind, and spirit.

—*Susanna Foth Aughtmon*

FAITH STEP: Pause and remember the first time you realized your Heavenly Father loves you and delights in you. Journal about it, or share the memory with someone who might need to hear it. ☙

Keeping Promises

The bridal party stood in front of us as we waited for the bride—Laura Lee, my future daughter-in-law—to walk down the aisle. You could hear a pin drop. My son Jordan shuffled his feet and glanced around, making it obvious to me that he was nervous. The wait felt unusually long.

My 88-year-old mother, who is hard of hearing yet has a great sense of humor, leaned over to me and said, too loudly, "Maybe she changed her mind."

I pretended I didn't hear her, so she leaned over again and said it even louder! The wedding party, those sitting nearby, and even Jordan laughed out loud. I watched Jordan's shoulders relax after the comic relief. Then the door opened, the music started, and Laura Lee walked down the aisle. I knew Jordan never once thought Laura Lee had changed her mind.

When Jordan and Laura Lee got engaged, my husband, Zane, and I spoke with them about how marriage is an example of God's enduring, promise-keeping love to us and reminded them to take their vows seriously. And they did. I may be biased, but they wrote the most beautiful, poetic, humorous, tender, and uplifting vows I've ever heard. They knew that of all the details that go into planning a wedding, none mattered as much as the promises they made to each other before God and others.

Marriage is not easy. When you enter into it making vows to stay despite the ups and downs that life hurls at you, I believe that gives you the best chance of success at long-term love. Married or not, most of us know that loving feelings can come and go in our personal relationships, but the ones that last are the ones where both people are committed to keeping their promises. In the same way, we know that our loving God will always keep His promises to us—and we can show our love to Him by honoring our faith commitments. In that way, we build a relationship that lasts a lifetime.

—*Jeannie Blackmer*

FAITH STEP: Choose one of the following, depending on your circumstances: Write your partner a love letter expressing your love for them and the promises you've vowed to keep. Alternatively, write a love letter to God describing your confidence in His love for you and your commitment to follow Him.

Note: Certainly, circumstances exist, such as abuse or unfaithfulness, where a marriage ends for the physical and mental health of one or both of the people involved. If you're in an abusive relationship, call the National Domestic Violence Hotline at 1-800-799-7233.

If I speak in the tongues of men or of angels, but do not have love, I am only a resounding gong or a clanging cymbal.

—1 Corinthians 13:1 (NIV)

I was 10 years old when I memorized 1 Corinthians 13 for a Sunday school class. We had to stand in front of our teacher and recite it. I think we got a sticker. It was a whole lot of memorizing for a sticker, but it was worth the effort. The words of this chapter have stuck with me all these years: Love is patient. Love is kind. Love doesn't envy.

One thing is for sure, memorizing the love chapter is a whole lot easier than living it out. I need more than a sticker to empower me to live out the life-altering words of this powerful passage of Scripture.

When my life is focused on me, it is hard to love other people. They often disagree with me. Or do things differently than I would like them to do. But living according to 1 Corinthians 13 means that I need God's love to change my heart to look like His. It needs to work itself down into the selfish nooks and crannies of my soul, changing my focus. When I invite God to do a love renovation in my life, I'm asking Him to help me see people the way He does, as precious and wholly loved. If I don't invite His love in, my life becomes a whole lot of empty noise. Let the love makeover begin.

—*Susanna Foth Aughtmon*

When Love Looks Different

I tried to be brave as I said goodbye to my son, a young adult who lived 900 miles from us. Our daughter had been a missionary for several years, so I was familiar with difficult goodbyes. This one, though, was different.

Jason had just gone through a significant loss. As I was attending a conference just a few hours from his city, I took advantage of the opportunity and traveled to see him. I wanted to encourage him in person after being heartbroken for him at a distance. Our time together was brief but just enough for me to shower him with love. I listened, empathized, and sat with him without providing pat answers I knew would not be helpful. I wanted to be a loving presence when his closest friends and family were far away.

I thought I handled the situation well until I started the long drive home. My heart still ached because the problem wasn't remedied. I started thinking about what I should have said and what I needed to tell him when I got home. Hours on the road gave me time to think of solutions that I believed would make him happy.

A few days after I returned home, I called Jason and shared the solutions I had devised. I was taken aback when he did not gratefully welcome my advice. Instead, he responded with, "I'll be fine, Mom. It's hard, but I'm OK."

It took me a few days to process the different experiences of being welcomed into his life but then later positioned on the sidelines. I felt rejected in my efforts to love him well.

Then God showed me, as I reflected on what Jason needed, that love is not always being in the same space with others or finding solutions to a loved one's problems. Instead, it may include being present when they need you to be and giving them autonomy for God to work in their lives.

I thought love was taking my son's pain away; it really was respecting the space he needed to move forward. This realization taught me that loving someone includes accepting different ways a person needs to be cared for—ones that *they* decide, not me. And that's OK.

—Brenda L. Yoder

Faith Step: Consider how your loved ones need to receive love from you. Ask God for creative ways to respond differently.

Making Time for Love

Payette Lake in McCall, Idaho, is a beautiful glacial lake carved out at the foot of the Payette National Forest. Last fall, my husband, Scott, and I made the 2-hour drive through the mountains to visit for our twenty-seventh anniversary weekend. We sipped coffee together, meandered through vintage stores, and had a fancy celebration dinner overlooking the lake. It was so fun, and it was a much-needed time together.

Scott and I have recognized the need to put time aside to focus on *us*. It is not just the quantity of time we spend together, but the intentionality of those moments.

Our love for each other has grown over the years. We like to laugh together. We cheer each other on and encourage each other in our faith. But it's not always easy. We have endured financial struggles. We've faced obstacles in our ministry and in raising a family of young men together.

If we let the busyness of life get in the way of our relationship, the ripple effect is felt in all areas of our lives. Communication suffers. We miss out on the important details in each other's days. We are disconnected. Spending time, just the two of us, whether we are celebrating by a beautiful lake or simply touching base at the end of the day, tethers our hearts to each other.

Love doesn't grow if you don't nurture it. This is true in my marriage and in my relationship with God. I need to intentionally set aside time to focus on Him. If I wander from His love, the ripple effect is felt across all areas of my life. Fear sets in. I worry about the future. I am disconnected from His voice. God invites me to draw near to Him, and He promises to draw near to me (James 4:8). He longs to spend time with me, to guide and correct me with His truth, and to show me His rich, unending grace when I make mistakes.

God's love for me is bigger than Lake Payette. It's taller than the mountains and deeper than the ocean. He loves me simply because I am His. I want to spend my life loving Him back. I want my heart to be tethered to His.

—*Susanna Foth Aughtmon*

FAITH STEP: Set aside time today to take a walk and focus on God's love for you. As you pray, thank Him for anchoring your life in His love.

Building Bridges

In my role as an elementary school counselor, I handle complicated situations with children who have significant behavioral issues or dysregulated emotions. To advocate for the students' needs, I must build bridges with parents, using empathy, understanding, and collaboration to get the right interventions for their child in place. It's refreshing and rewarding when we reach the end goal of doing what's best for the child despite obstacles or differences of opinions or beliefs.

Because I engage in this collaborative work so often at school, I get easily irritated when such understanding and cooperation are absent in personal situations where there is less at stake. Whether it's my marriage or other relationships, I have similar expectations for healthy communication with the people I volunteer with.

This is why I was frustrated when taking on a new role with a friend, Jamie. I hadn't worked closely with her before, and her communication style felt controlling and stifling in a way I'd never experienced from her. I found my anxiety rising with each email I opened from Jamie. While at work I had well-developed techniques for dealing with difficult individuals, in my personal life I had little capacity to deal with such interactions.

As my frustration grew, I was tempted to speak directly to Jamie about the situation. Then a few other people shared that they had similar experiences with her. I realized the way she was communicating wasn't personal or aimed specifically at me; it was simply an aspect of her personality I'd never encountered before. I also knew she would be crushed if I confronted her or if she knew her behavior had negatively affected others.

I prayed about the situation. I sensed God wanted me to work with Him to overcome my frustration and angst rather than being confrontational. He helped me reflect on what I knew about her private circumstances. Could wounds in Jamie's personal life spill into how she related to others? I realized if I could build bridges with parents I disagreed with, I could also do so with a friend. I began seeking God's counsel and that of another trusted leader to gently guide Jamie without compromising the tasks of our mutual work.

God showed me that empathy and understanding build bridges in all relationships, even when I struggle with them. The point when it becomes a struggle is exactly when I must surrender to God's love. I'm still working on loving others with God's eyes and heart rather than my own, but I'm learning to trust the process.

—Brenda L. Yoder

FAITH STEP: If you're frustrated with someone, pause before you respond. Take a minute to ask God to first fill you with His love.

For I am convinced that neither death nor life, neither angels nor demons, neither the present nor the future, nor any powers, neither height nor depth, nor anything else in all creation, will be able to separate us from the love of God that is in Christ Jesus our Lord.

—Romans 8:38–39 (NIV)

When Paul wrote this letter to the Christians in Rome, he had been persecuted in countless ways—whipped, beaten, imprisoned, flogged, left for dead, plotted against multiple times. But even in the midst of life-or-death struggles, he knew nothing he endured in this life could ever separate him from God's love. That included his own mistakes.

Jesus loved us so much He would have rather died than leave us in the dark. His mercy is unfathomable, His grace indescribable, and His forgiveness encompasses a distance greater than the east is from the west.

Can Jesus forgive addiction? Absolutely.

Can Jesus forgive adultery? Without a doubt.

Can Jesus forgive bad attitudes and bitterness? Of course.

Can Jesus forgive the backslidden, the judgmental, the lukewarm Christian, the legalist, or the people who speak harshly when they should be kind? Yes, yes, yes, yes, and yes.

He can and He has.

For the contaminated, He washes away the grime until we're whiter than snow. For the broken, He binds up our wounds. For the empty, He fills us. For the hurting, He soothes. For the tattered heart, He sews it back with threads of grace. For the rejected, He embraces us. For the fallen, He lifts us back to our feet. For the depressed, He gives hope. For the unwanted, He adopts. For the weary, He gives rest. For the unlovable, He says, "I love you."

In the words of Betsie ten Boom, "There is no pit so deep that God's love is not deeper still."

—Tara Johnson

CHAPTER 3

Personal Growth

We Don't Have to Prove Ourselves

L ook how tattered it is," Sara said, nudging me and pointing to our friend Claire's Bible. Tattered was generous. Those pages were on the brink of disintegration, looking like the actual Dead Sea Scrolls.

But she wasn't being mean. On the contrary—at Bible study, a well-worn Bible was a badge of honor. It served the same purpose as donning scuffed, rumpled leather boots at a cowboy convention. Cred. Proof that you are who you say you are. Cowboys wrangle and work outside. Their boots attest. Christians read their Bibles. Rumpled pages attest.

"A Bible on its last legs," Sara added, smiling. Then she pointed to her own. "Mine's getting close to that!" She was right. Both ladies' Bibles looked as if they'd been around since Moses himself. I glanced down at my Bible. Two weeks ago, I'd treated myself to a crisp new one, after the purse-sized copy I'd had since college finally busted in two. (Also, the letters seemed to have shrunk over time. Certainly it was the print size that had changed over 20 years, not my vision.)

The discrepancy in our Bibles' conditions was stark. Most of my pages were still stuck together. I suddenly felt the need to announce that I, too, had a Bible more weathered than a 100-year-old cattleman.

I opened my mouth to speak, but then I closed it again.

Something about needing the validation of people knowing I *have* a worn Bible struck me as ironic. I was chasing affirmation from people, rather than the God I sought through His Word.

That feeling of needing to prove myself to the people around me wasn't new. I've had many similar experiences in parenting, work, and everyday conversations: biting my tongue when I'd realized that I'm on a path of self-validation, trying to make sure the people around me know that I am competent, cool, experienced. I had to remind myself that my willingness to *not speak* self-justifying words says more about my maturity.

Maybe you can relate?

Have you listened for the Holy Spirit's nudge when you've felt the need to prove yourself to people? He reminds us that in the big things and the small God sees, He knows, and He is with us. He knows when you seek Him. He knows your heart better than anyone. What's better than the God of the universe acknowledging our hearts' devotion and good work?

Every time we stop working to prove ourselves to people, we can share a smile and a wink with our Heavenly Father who knows and sees all things.

—*Molly DeFrank*

FAITH STEP: Call to mind an area where you have felt misunderstood or unrecognized. Pray, "Lord, You see my heart. You know me. Your approval is more than enough for me."

When the Wind Blows

When we lived on the top of a mesa, we sometimes experienced tremendous winds. Our house rattled and shook and tumbleweeds blew into our yard. The flowers in our gardens bent, almost touching the ground, with the powerful gusts.

I worried about the wind destroying my gardens, so I researched online about what to do and learned that wind actually works magic for plants. Each time a plant is pushed by the wind, it releases a hormone called auxin, which makes the stem stronger. I didn't need to do anything but let the wind do the work.

Similar to the plant world, when we endure trials, we also grow stronger. Some of the toughest times in my life were the 7 years my middle son was drinking. I had no power over his choices. I had to let go of any sense of control over his life and, like the wind with my plants, let God do the work. To help me, I regularly attended Al-Anon meetings, a recovery program similar to Alcoholics Anonymous but for those who love an addict. It wasn't easy, but the growth from the difficult journey of learning to trust a loving God made me stronger. I discovered an unexplainable peace that sustained me even when I didn't know where my son was or how he was doing. I found people in similar situations who inspired me. My mantra became "I can't. God can. I think I'll let Him."

Thankfully, my son is now sober, and he helps other alcoholics find sobriety. Inspired by my son's efforts to use knowledge gained from his painful season, I also share my experience to provide strength to others living with or loving an addict.

When we face a windstorm in life, a trial that tests our faith, placing our total trust in a power bigger than us works magic for our souls. Trusting God and not giving up, even in the midst of suffering, will make us stronger—a strength even a raging windstorm cannot break.

—Jeannie Blackmer

FAITH STEP: How has persevering through a trial in your life made you stronger? Write about this in your journal or contemplate it as you go about your day. ✒

Bravery by Degrees

A few years ago, my little grandson, Eli, taught me a big lesson about bravery.

Our family went on vacation to a lovely resort in the Florida panhandle. Eli loves the water, so we headed down to the pool. He wanted to go in but was terrified of letting go of Mimi (me), Mommy, or whoever was with him.

Eli had on one of those yellow floatie rings that go over the head, buckling underneath. There was *zero* possibility of him sinking, but he didn't believe it.

Clinging close, lips quivering, he said, "Mimi! Don't let me go, Mimi!"

"You're all right, baby. Mimi's got you."

Bit by bit, I convinced him to grab my neck. He held on tight but cried out in fear if I encouraged him to let go. I reminded him all along, "Mimi's right here. You're OK, buddy." But he wasn't buying it.

As the morning continued and as he watched other kids jumping and frolicking in the pool, he mustered enough courage to let go of my hands. We clapped and high-fived his bravery, smiling big when he declared, "I floating, Mimi!" "Yes, you are, buddy. Yes, you are."

The next obstacle was jumping off the side of the pool into Daddy's arms. Daddy held his little hands and let him jump. "Catch me, Daddy, catch me!" "I'll catch you, Son."

Little by little, degree by degree, Eli's bravery grew. After 4 days at the pool, he could float on his tummy, flip onto his back, and paddle about without holding Daddy's hands.

Aren't we all like that sometimes? Jesus asks us to jump, assuring us He'll catch us. But we balk. We fear, negotiate, and doubt. We lay out our conditions, and all along our Daddy is right there, arms extended, ready to catch us if we trust enough to jump.

We take a tiny jump to test Him. Will He really catch us? But our trust deepens, and we achieve bravery by degrees, courage by inches, and eventually, total trust. "For God has not given us a spirit of fear, but of power and of love and of a sound mind" (2 Timothy 1:7, NKJV).

When we swim out and into the deep water of God's purpose for our lives, we can safely float, certain He is with us and will never forsake us. And as we float, our Father claps, high-fives, and smiles big.

—*Kate Battistelli*

Faith Step: Is there a big step you've been wanting to take in your life that you've been avoiding because it scares you? Close your eyes and imagine God ready to catch you if you stumble. Then go out and take that step.

…for one's life does not consist in the abundance of his possessions.

—Luke 12:15 (ESV)

After losing all our possessions except for the clothes on our backs in a raging wildfire, we discovered that life truly does not consist in the abundance of possessions. However, there were some essentials we did need to buy right away, such as underwear.

I went to T. J. Maxx, a store that often sells merchandise at a discount, sometimes due to a defect. I found a cute box of men's underwear from the Life is Good brand. This American apparel and accessories company is known for its stick figure named Jake and its simple, optimistic message that life is good.

My husband, Zane, opened the box to take a look and found the defect. Instead of the words "Life is Good" written on the waistband, it said "Life is God." We laughed, because this is one of the lessons we had been learning through our loss—that a good life is not based on possessions.

God does have a sense of humor. I love how He continues to remind me that life is all about being in a relationship with Him and with those we love. Our recovery from the fire is still ongoing, but as we gradually replace our lost stuff, I'll keep in mind that Life is God.

—Jeannie Blackmer

Wonderfully Made

Before our first child was born, my husband and I transformed a spare bedroom into a beautiful, animal-themed nursery. He assembled a crib and hand-painted a mural on one wall. I ironed curtains, washed bedding, and created custom accents to match the color scheme. Before the room was complete, I stenciled Psalm 139:13–14 (NIV) just above the crib: "For you created my inmost being; you knit me together in my mother's womb. I praise you because I am fearfully and wonderfully made."

Every day that I rocked one of my babies to sleep in the nursery, the words jumped off the wall and into my soul. I prayed for my children to grow into the potential God placed within them. I prayed Gideon would become a spiritual mighty warrior, just like his namesake in the Bible. I prayed Canaan would bring joy, respite, and hope to others, like the Promised Land did for the Israelites. I prayed that Adelle—named after *adelphe,* the New Testament Greek word for *sister*—would indeed become a sister-in-Christ to others and live her life for Him. And I asked the Lord to bless Solomon with the same wisdom He had once granted the king.

As they grew, I watched my children's potential unfold like a spring bud, just as I had prayed. Later, when the last baby outgrew the crib and the nursery begged for a makeover, I hesitated before painting over the Bible verse. I sat in the rocking chair one last time—noticing that it had lost padding over the years while I had gained it—and stared up at the words that I had written for my children but that had been etched into my own heart.

Could those words still apply to me? I wondered. They were easy to believe for my children, whose lives were just beginning, but much harder to accept when I looked in the mirror. Then I remembered the passage had not been written about a sleeping baby, but about a man, King David, who was reflecting on his complex life walking with the Lord. He'd been through war and peace, sin and repentance, love and loss, wisdom and foolishness. Yet he knew he was still "wonderfully made," flaws and all.

I grabbed a paintbrush and smiled. I was longer hesitant to paint over the verse, because its truth was now written on my heart. Time and age had not erased my potential.

—Emily E. Ryan

FAITH STEP: Write out Psalm 139:13–14 and tape it to your bathroom mirror. Whenever you read it, think about all the ways it applies to you in that moment. ✒

Life Hacks

A recent trend that I hope sticks around for a while is "I was today years old when I learned…" These "life hack" discoveries can be as simple as better ways to keep the end of the tube of toothpaste fresh or as life altering as saving hundreds of dollars on insurance if your car is equipped with automatic braking.

I was today years old when I realized I could get a better cell signal if I switch my phone to airplane mode, which forces the phone to search for any available tower. I was today years old when I heard that pressing a hot spoon against a mosquito bite will help reduce the sting, swelling, and itch. Who knew?

The bizarre hacks are worth a try. Some science-like person discovered that if you chew the same flavor of gum when you take a test that you did when studying for the test, you'll remember more. Really? I may need to repeat high school to find out if that's true.

I was today years old when I read that lip balm can soothe a paper cut and that a dry tea bag slipped into shoes will help absorb odors.

But I was (mumble, mumble) years old when I realized that opting for what God says is always the best choice. What a great life hack. Saves time and energy, soothes headaches, and eliminates regret.

If Jesus says, "Pray for those who are unkind to you," why would I waste time wondering how to handle the situation?

If the biblical advice is "don't repay evil for evil," it's guaranteed to work like magic.

If evidence of a life lived His way is "love, joy, peace, patience, kindness, goodness, faithfulness, gentleness, and self-control" (Galatians 5:22–23, NLT), that covers most situations I'll face, doesn't it? How am I going to make this paper cut in our relationship heal? Apply a little love to it. A little extra kindness. How will I handle this uncomfortable situation at work? With gentleness and patience.

God has a life hack for everything. Literally.

—Cynthia Ruchti

FAITH STEP: When your power cords get tangled, empty toilet paper rolls or clam clips will do the trick. But when the threads of your life get messy, God's supernatural life hacks are there for you. Create your own list of life hacks based on what you know God says and what aligns with His plan for His children.

Walking with God

My three dogs, all different breeds and ages, keep me hopping when I take them for a walk around the neighborhood. It's not an easy task. Trying to keep dogs with varying temperaments in pace can be tricky, but God has used them to teach me a lot about myself and my relationship with Him.

Brieanne is an 8-month-old blue heeler and is as strong as an ox. She's solid muscle and pure energy. All that baby girl wants to do is run. She's enthusiastic about everything. Dirt. Squirrels. Birds. Trash. Her goal is to get to the next thing as quickly as possible. When a car zooms by, she lunges and pulls, pants and slobbers, with no concept of the possible danger. She's happy but impulsive. If I let her have her way, she'd be dead in a heartbeat.

I've been that way often in my walk with God. Always straining to push past His will. Resisting His gentle tugs. *Wait, Tara. Be still.*

Then there's Elvis, a 10-year-old poodle mix. Elvis is pretty easy to walk most of the time until…*boom!* He wants something. Whether it's an interesting smell or a trail he's never explored, once that dog's mind is made up, he will not budge. He stubbornly digs his paws into the ground, bucking against the leash like a mule.

I can relate. I follow God until His plan bumps into mine. Then I buck. I dig in my heels. That's when God has to correct me and get me back on the right track again.

Finally, there's Sugar. She's a bichon frise, 10 pounds, 15 years old, completely deaf and mostly blind. The poor thing is riddled with arthritis and touches of doggie dementia. She can no longer wear a leash because she chokes easily, but she adores walking. She follows my shadow, keeping pace with my steps. Wherever I go, she goes. Her inability to hear doesn't concern her as long as she can see the outline of my presence. The few times she has lagged behind, I pick her up and carry her the rest of the way.

I want to be like Sugar. Following in my Savior's shadow. Keeping pace with His every move, His touch, His heartbeat.

Sugar and I get each other. We've been walking together for a long time. Maybe that's the secret. A relationship forged in time and trust. That's what I want with Jesus.

—*Tara Johnson*

Faith Step: Write down pivotal moments in your life (births, deaths, challenges, and changes) and reflect on the decisions that followed. Did you try to rush ahead of God's timing, did you buck the changes, or did you walk in step with God? Look for areas where you'd like to improve in the future and ask Him to help you going forward.

Trust in the LORD *with all your heart and lean not on your own understanding; in all your ways submit to him, and he will make your paths straight.*

—PROVERBS 3:5–6 (NIV)

On my first walk of the new year, I discovered a new trail in my neighborhood tucked away behind a row of houses and shaded by mature, overgrown trees. The trail itself was paved and roomy, a straight shot from start to finish. The creek beside the trail, however, was not. It twisted and turned, hugging the trail and then abandoning it, with no patterns or predictability whatsoever.

I thought about the metaphorical paths mentioned in Proverbs 3:5–6 and quickly concluded that mine were more like the creek than the trail. I often prayed for a straight shot to wisdom and discernment, but I always seemed to meander rather than march. Why did life contain so many plot twists when the Lord promised straight paths?

Later, I looked up the word *paths* in the original language. Apparently, a path can refer to a road, a way of living, or the traveler himself. I had been so concerned about the Lord straightening out the events of my life, I never considered that perhaps He is more concerned with straightening my heart and soul. Maybe the twists and turns that life takes are actually the most direct way to living a deeper relationship with the Lord.

I returned to the path by my house and walked between the creek and the trail, thanking God for the reminder that He cares more about who I'm becoming and what I'm learning about Him than where I'm going.

—Emily E. Ryan

Learning New Hard Things

y husband taught higher-level math for more than 30 years. He has an effortless sense of computing numbers. I, on the other hand, do not.

That's why I was somewhat stressed when my school counseling coworker and I had to submit very specific numerical data when we were applying for a certified school counseling program. The required data differed from the typical percentages we used to show student growth based on interventions we implemented. It was a statistical formula I didn't understand.

I didn't want to pass my portion of the project off to my younger coworker because I was incapable. I prayed that God would help me use the same perseverance and problem-solving skills I use with students and in my job as an author to tackle this problem.

I started by telling myself that I can do hard things—a mindset I often teach students. Kids can feel inadequate or overwhelmed when they struggle or don't understand something. They often shut down or avoid the task entirely. They become empowered when they realize they're capable of doing tasks that once felt uncomfortable or even impossible.

I employed the same strategies I would use when coaching a student. My coworker showed me the steps needed to assign our data to the prescribed formula. Though I followed the steps, I understood the process differently. On my own, I did calculations in a way I understood. I plugged them into the formula and was encouraged when I got the same answer as my coworker, though my process was longer.

It took me a while to get all the statistics compiled for our program application, but when I finished, I felt more accomplished than I had in a long time. Remembering the problem-solving strengths God gave me fueled the confidence to learn something new, even though it was hard. Instead of ruminating on my weaknesses, I believed I could understand and apply something I hadn't done before. And it worked!

—*Brenda L. Yoder*

Faith Step: Are you facing a challenging situation? Ask God to show you where you have persevered and succeeded in doing something hard in the past. Apply the same tenacity, confidence, or problem-solving strategies to what lies before you.

Growing from Seed

oday I received the most wonderful magazine in the mail—the Baker Creek Heirloom Seed Company catalog. My husband, Scott, gets nervous when I start looking at catalogs. He knows I have big plans. Each glossy page is covered with delightful offerings, from bee balm to heirloom tomatoes. I marked the veggies and flowers that I want to incorporate in this spring's planting. The beginnings of my garden dreams are held in those pages.

When we moved into our new house 4 years ago, our yard was a blank slate. My mom and dad drove from Colorado to Idaho with three beautiful Annabelle hydrangeas soaking in a plastic kid's pool in the back of their SUV. Seeing them planted in an alcove next to my front door gave me more joy than I thought possible. My mom says that's the day I became a small farmer.

There is something miraculous about watching something grow from a seed into a full-fledged plant. This winter I could hardly wait for spring. I was going to plant snap peas. After the last frost, I added organic compost to the planting mix and poked holes in the soil. I lined up each seed next to a small metal trellis. I was creating the perfect conditions for the peas to grow in.

Each day, the soaker hose watered the soil. I anxiously awaited the plants' arrival. Within a month, the tiny seeds that had been pressed inches deep into the soil began sprouting. Within 2 months, they were wrapping themselves around the trellis and forming seedpods. The snap peas never made it to the table. I ate them straight off the vine. They were delicious.

In my perfect world, growth would be consistent. But, like my snap peas, my personal growth doesn't come quickly, and it requires work. I can't grow on my own. God has to nurture His seeds of goodness within me—things like patience, kindness, and self-control. He is bringing about the right conditions, the right people, and the right opportunities for me to produce my best fruit. He is the Good Farmer, and He knows exactly how to help me grow into the person He created me to be.

—Susanna Foth Aughtmon

FAITH STEP: Where in your life do you want to see growth this year? Share your struggles and hopes with God. Pray and ask Him to grow you into the person He created you to be.

Forget the former things;
do not dwell on the past.

—Isaiah 43:18 (NIV)

I don't use the Notes app on my phone the way it was intended. Oh, I take notes on it all the time, but too often I neglect to go back to implement the notes.

Today, moved by a sudden, unexplained urgency to see what I might have missed, I found a Christmas list from years ago, a reminder to purchase a roll of masking tape (perhaps in another decade), various book ideas that now seem like gibberish, the lyrics of an especially meaningful worship song, and some "color" words that sound like paint swatches I must have been considering for the dining room. Driftwood Gray. Mist-on-the-Moors. Not Beige.

I lingered over a quote I either created or heard but failed to note from whom: "I spent so much time rehearsing my past, I had no voice left for discussing my possibilities."

I'd been tired, bordering on exhausted, when I recorded that quote. For weeks, I'd slogged through life. My normal energy had taken a vacation, apparently, and left me with lethargy as a companion. Not surprisingly, that affected where my thoughts hovered—subconsciously rehearsing every wrong thing I'd ever done. Every unwise word. Every dumb decision. Clear back to foolish things I did when I was five years old. What?

In the time between recording that note and today, leaning more and more into the truths of God and His Word, I've learned you can't climb out of exhaustion on the back of past regrets. Even before Jesus arrived to make a way for forgiveness, God said, "Forget the former things; do not dwell on the past."

I should put *that* in my Notes app.

—Cynthia Ruchti

Hope Doesn't Gather Dust

I must have missed the memo that we're supposed to pull furniture away from the wall occasionally to dust back there. When a grandchild lost a beloved toy under the couch, moving it couldn't be avoided. By knee and muscle and a touch of stubborn determination, I inched the beast away from the wall.

When anything stands still for that long, it can't help but gather dust.

I could have made enough money for a nice vacation if bags of dust held any value. Even dryer lint has more purpose than dust! Lint apparently makes a great fire starter, compost, and worm farm material. Dust has no real value except as a clue that cleaning behind heavy things isn't my strong suit.

How could God have known (rhetorical question) I'd need the reminder in a video that asked, "Is your hope gathering dust?"

When my focus is on circumstances rather than God's power, an almost imperceptible (at first) weight of concern can settle on me like little flakes of dust. Those motes are the beginning of what can become a blizzard of worry. My *hope* can't afford to gather dust any more than my Bible can. (Have you, like me, sometimes asked, "Now, where did I put that? Oh. Still in the tote bag I took to church last week.")

When my hope is alive, vibrant, and hard at work rather than sitting there gathering dust, it—a beautiful gift from God—not only helps me cope with life's concerns but also keeps me moving forward despite the doubts and worries that weigh me down.

Hope needs to keep moving. It needs to keep breathing, exercising its muscles, showing up rather than sitting in a corner untouched. Sometimes that means repeating what I know to be true about God until confidence returns. Sometimes that means turning to God's Word rather than to an unhealthy habit (hello, gluten-free Oreos).

Hope likes to be let out as much as a puppy eager for sunshine. I "let it out" when I give it attention, give God attention, and take my eyes off the staring contest with my concerns.

Over the past few months of watching my mother-in-law struggle with her failing 93-year-old body, finances taking a hit (when isn't that true?), and grandchildren flirting with decisions that can only lead to regret, my hope was starting to get weighed down. Life's circumstances—and a friendly reminder from God—required me to haul it from storage and put it into action. A couch, a video, God's Word. All with the same message. May I ever live with hope that gathers no dust.

—*Cynthia Ruchti*

Faith Step: Do you have a sign, painting, or other decoration in your house that includes or represents hope? You might want to watch for one at a thrift store. Take a cleaning rag to it as a reminder to keep your heart's hope from gathering dust. ❧

Invest in Yourself

A few years ago, I began thinking about enrolling in an online program to get my teaching certificate. I was already teaching at a private school, but the certificate would allow me to teach in a public school and, hopefully, open the doors for more ministry opportunities. The only thing holding me back from enrolling was the cost of the course.

For Christmas, my in-laws gave us each a few hundred dollars, as they did every year. I usually tucked the money in my wallet to use throughout the year on impulse buys like clothes, shoes, movies, or books, but this year I used the entire amount to sign up for the teaching program. It was a long and challenging commitment, with months of projects, tests, observations, and papers that tested my faith daily. A few times I wondered if I had made a mistake, but I pushed through because I didn't want to waste the money I'd invested. By the next fall, I not only had my teaching certificate, but I also had a new job in the same public school district that my own children attended.

Later, I told my father-in-law what a blessing the Christmas money had been. With my increase in salary, the few hundred dollars they had given me had essentially been multiplied by thirty. It was the best return on investment I'd ever experienced. He smiled, and I could tell he was doing some mental calculations. "Actually," he corrected me, "that's just a 1-year return. If you continue teaching, that return will be annual."

He was right. It was the first time I had ever taken a leap of faith and invested in myself in such a significant way, and the experience had stretched me spiritually and grown my faith significantly. The financial gains were certainly exciting, but the greatest benefit was the knowledge that I could accomplish a difficult long-term goal. It inspired me to look for other ways I could challenge myself in the future and more creative opportunities to invest—rather than spend—a portion of my money on personal growth every year.

—*Emily E. Ryan*

Faith Step: Whether it's learning a new skill, joining a Bible study, or buying new running shoes, take a leap of faith and set aside a small portion of your budget to invest in an activity that will stretch you spiritually and help you grow.

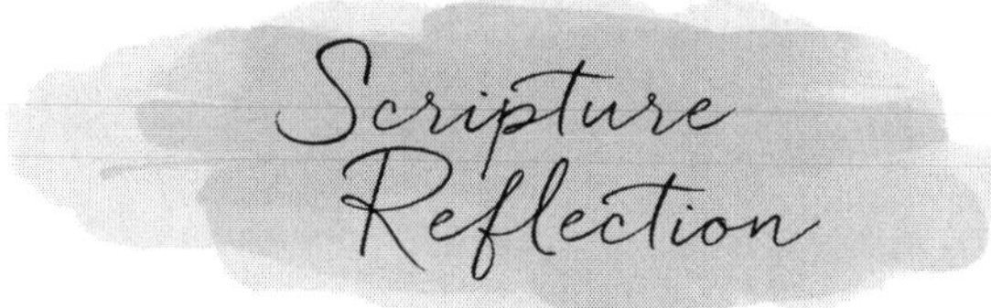

Do not fear, for I have redeemed you; I have summoned you by name; you are mine.

—Isaiah 43:1 (NIV)

We all have scars—marks that remind us of what we survived, albeit painfully, and how far God was willing to go to rescue and heal us.

If we aren't careful, we may believe our flaws will forever mark us. Thankfully, our struggles don't define our worth. Instead, they become the guideposts to remind us what God has brought us through. Just like the great heroes of faith, He takes nobodies and transforms them into somebodies. In that way, all the stories in the Bible are our own.

I am Jonah. I often buck God's plans when His agenda doesn't match mine.

I am Daniel. I live in a land that wants to change my identity.

I am Eve. I long for the forbidden, and my mistakes don't only hurt me but also countless others.

I am Peter. I struggle to keep my eyes on Jesus.

I am Moses. I often feel I'm inadequate.

I am Esther. Even when I can't see the big picture, God has set me in this moment for a special purpose.

I am scarred yet lavishly loved, broken yet treasured. I was chained but am now free. I am redeemed. I am loved.

Your story is so much better than any fairy tale, romance, mystery, or adventure saga. You have been fought for by the God of the universe. With each beat of your heart, He is drawing you to Him. Always calling.

I love you.

—*Tara Johnson*

Self-Care

The Beauty of Broken

My son and I were coloring one rainy day, and I frowned when my red crayon snapped with a pop. "Oh, man! I pressed too hard. My crayon just snapped in half."

Nate looked up with a dimpled grin. "It's OK, Momma. The great thing about crayons is that they still color no matter how broken they are."

We then composed a list of all the things that are better when they are broken.

Peanuts are hard to eat until we break the shell. Shoes hurt like crazy until we break them in. What's the fun of a water balloon that doesn't pop? Or a piñata that still holds its candy? Eggshells have to be broken to make a cheese omelet, and glow sticks won't shine until they are snapped.

Our culture has glamorized what the world defines as "perfect." From the airbrushed models gracing the latest magazine covers to the highlight reels inundating social media, we are constantly told we must be flawless to be accepted. The flip side of that lie is that anything broken must be rejected.

The more that we build our identity on something other than Christ—whether it's our appearance, social reputation, prestige, or approval from others—the greater the pain when that identity crumbles.

Approval and love are not the same thing. Neither are brokenness and a lack of worth.

God loves to use broken things. It takes broken soil to produce a crop and broken bread to feed hungry mouths. Just like the woman who anointed Jesus's feet, alabaster boxes can be broken to release the sweet aroma of perfume.

All my life, I've heard it said that broken things are special because the cracks allow the light to come in. I'm not sure that's true. For God's kids, brokenness allows the Light to shine out.

I recently dropped my cell phone, and now its glass face is a spider web of cracks. Yet its broken exterior hasn't affected its ability to function one iota. It's chock-full of pictures, videos, memories, and a hundred other treasures. Just because it's broken doesn't mean I need to throw it away. I wouldn't part with what's inside for a million dollars.

We're all broken, but our worth is immeasurable. Some might say we're all the more interesting because of our flaws.

—Tara Johnson

FAITH STEP: Make a list of the "broken places" that make you unique. In what ways could you use these as a way to minister to others? ✦

God Wants Rest *for* You, Not *from* You

Is it cancer? Am I dying?" I searched the doctor's face. This was the second time I'd been to the ER in a month for chest pain.

"No. All your tests are clear. It's anxiety," he said. "Sometimes anxiety can cause chest pain, and we've ruled everything else out."

"Anxiety?" I was certain that this doc was about to diagnose me with a rare disease.

"Do you have any underlying stress in your life right now?" he asked.

Underlying stress? Do four kids under six, a new house, and an upcoming camping trip count? Stress was my middle name.

"Well, yes."

"Would you like a sedative?" he offered.

"Well, I have to go home to wrangle children, move the wash to the dryer before it molds, create a meal plan for the week, and then pack for a camping trip. I'm too busy for a sedative, Doc."

"OK," he said, making a note in his chart.

I couldn't believe that my worry was causing literal pain in my chest and down my arm. I *wanted* to slow down. Breaks sounded nice—hypothetically. But there was too much left unfinished every day. There was too much work that wasn't even *started* each day. Shouldn't I keep going until it's all tied in a neat little bow? Shouldn't I finish the work before I take a break?

For so long I had rejected this counterintuitive idea of rest amidst chaos. Whose idea was rest, anyway?

Another voice in my mind responded, *Ahem. It was God's idea. God's literal commandment.* Jesus shed more light on this command, reminding us that a day of rest was made *for us,* for our benefit.

Obeying His call to rest is a way to show that we trust God. We trust that His purposes will be accomplished even while we rest. God's work is neither slowed nor hindered by our sitting down to eat lunch, sleeping a full night, or taking a moment to breathe. This truth is obvious to our minds, but our hearts often miss the memo. His work continues, and our hearts experience true peace—when we trust Him.

—*Molly DeFrank*

Faith Step: Pray as you respond to His call to rest. "Lord, I have so much on my plate. I trust that You are working, even as I sleep, sit, and eat. I can rest without anxiety because You are always working."

Salon for the Soul

"How's the temperature?" Deah asked as the warm water seeped into my thick hair.

"Perfect," I said and closed my eyes, allowing myself to sink farther into the soft, padded salon chair. Deah is a friend from church with an innate sense of style and grace, so when she told me she had renewed her cosmetology license and gotten a job at a new salon, I knew I wanted to benefit from her services.

What I didn't know then was that a salon visit with Deah involved so much more than just a haircut. Every stylist is also trained in the fine art of scalp and neck massaging, so the shampoo and conditioning before the cut and style is more like 15 minutes of pure pampering. I smiled as Deah's fingers began working their magic and breathed in the refreshing aroma of luxury shampoo. The tension and stress that had built up from a hard week at work disappeared down the drain.

Later, after the cut, color, glaze, and blow dry, I shook my head gently from side to side and surveyed every angle of Deah's handiwork in the mirror. I loved how my hair felt lighter and healthier, as if it had been pruned for growth as one prunes a grapevine. I felt pruned for growth as well, amazed by how my time at the salon had given me the energy and confidence I needed to face the rest of my difficult week.

Deah moved away the following year, but I still return to the salon every 6 months for a little chair time. This year, I brought my tween daughter, Adelle, with me and treated her to her first "fancy" haircut. She was about to begin her second year at a challenging magnet school for gifted learners, and I knew she'd benefit from a boost in energy and confidence. With each step in the pampering process, I watched her face light up more and more until she was practically beaming with her new do by the time we left. "Thank you for taking me!" she said with a hug. "Can we do this again next year?"

I smiled and silently thanked God for the mother-daughter memory. "Absolutely!"

—*Emily E. Ryan*

FAITH STEP: Self-care can mean many things for many people. Where do you go when you need a boost in energy for a challenging week? And how might you incorporate activities to nourish your soul, like listening to worship music, praying, or reading the Bible?

How fair is your love, my sister, my spouse! How much better than wine is your love, and the scent of your perfumes than all spices!

—Song of Solomon 4:10 (NKJV)

Why should you expect a single good thing? You're nothing, you're nobody.

Thoughts of unworthiness make a loud noise in my head. How do I quiet their shout and relentless pounding in my soul?

The narrative of negative self-talk played in my head my entire life until Jesus came along and began writing a different script. Everything within me wanted to tell Him, "It's not true!" But how do you call God a liar? If He calls you beautiful, you are. If He calls you His masterpiece, how can you not be?

His light pours through our scars, overflowing as He whispers, "I have chosen you. Yes, you. You don't believe I would, but I do. I see you crouching in the back so no one sees your tears."

From the foundation of the world, before we were in our mothers' wombs, no matter what we've done, heard, been told, or believed, the truth is: *We are worthy.* Worthy of His love and worthy to be His bride, carrying His message to others who need truth, not the lie they've been fed. His light pours through our scars to shine His truth. Today, *you* are worthy of His love.

—Kate Battistelli

Refresh

Despite the conscious choice my husband and I make to spend evenings together rather than in meetings or other engagements, last night an important task took him away from home after supper. As he was grabbing his coat, he asked, "Do you want me to leave the TV on?"

"No!" I was surprised by my own exuberance. It made me realize that I'd grown to crave and be grateful for quiet as night descended. I wasn't engulfed by loneliness or a need to stay busy. Rather, I leaned into the wonder of a still evening in front of the fire.

Opting for quiet was a partial response to my yearlong focus on the word *refresh*. I'd embarked on a 12-month adventure of exploring that word and what it might mean for me. The first discovery was a sobering one—how little I sought to refresh myself in favor of serving others. I filled my days and hours with "meaningful" activity that had drained me of energy—and a clear understanding of *meaningful*.

Refresh. Reset. Reboot. Restore. The kinds of activities that I normally associated with those words—a lazy, restful week at the beach, a leisurely train trip through the Canadian Rockies, or a day-long spa treatment—weren't possible. Not at the moment. But a quieted heart and a glowing fire and my favorite tea? That I could manage. I began seeking other ways to restore myself. Music is like a nightlight for my soul, so I'm choosing music above fitting in one more project before day's end. Soft light invigorates, so I'm keeping my battery-operated waxlike candles lit, and I'm budgeting for more batteries.

 Inspired by Faith

Too often, refreshing is the last thing on my list. No. It's actually not on the list at all. But that's what this yearlong journey is showing me. The peace that comes from seeking quiet time won't come knocking at my door. It stands at the end of the driveway, hoping I'll invite it in.

I'm learning not to wave at it in passing, not to nod my head at how beautiful refreshment looks from afar, but to instead go out to meet it, to consciously make space for it, and to say no to the activities that would crowd it out rather than the other way around.

Refreshment won't come looking for me. It waits for me to notice the ways and the times I can invite it in.

—*Cynthia Ruchti*

Faith Step: What most invigorates you? Gardens, hikes, reading, time with friends, candlelight, or some other type of activity that is uniquely yours? Will you join me in making refreshing the soul a priority?

The Bluebird

The poor bluebird living above our basketball goal is a pitiful thing. Every morning, I walk outside to see my husband's driver's side rearview mirror battered and smeared, evidence of another early morning fight.

It would be funny if it weren't so sad.

My bluebird friend perches in front of my husband's rearview mirror and sees *him*. That vile, evil threat. Another male bluebird just like him. A threat to his family and home. So he does what must be done. He pecks the foul fowl until his head is nearly smashed flat and his beak resembles the blunt end of a hammer. Poor bluebird. He doesn't realize he's actually fighting his own reflection.

He's his own worst enemy. I shouldn't judge. I'm my own worst enemy too.

Too often, I base my decisions on how I feel. Every decision we make is based on either love or fear, and when those emotions get involved, I tend to veer toward being fearful. Bad choices are always the result.

That's the funny thing about emotions. They tell us because we feel a certain way, it must be so. We *feel* God doesn't love us due to circumstances beyond our control; therefore it must be *true* that God doesn't love us. We feel neglected by our spouse; therefore we are neglected. We feel hopeless in our circumstances; therefore there must not be hope.

Just like my bluebird buddy, we see something that looks real, so therefore it must be real.

Emotions are not good or bad. They just *are*. They are God-given ways of experiencing life in a profound way. But the blunt truth is this: our emotions usually have very little to do with reality. They swing and dive with alarming speed. Truth doesn't. God stays the same day in and day out. When in doubt, we must rely on His Word and not on how we feel.

My bluebird has taught me one of the greatest things I can do when battling fear—or any overwhelming feeling—is to cling to what I know, not how I feel. It makes all the difference, not just in how I manage my days but in how I live my life.

—*Tara Johnson*

Faith Step: When struggling with swinging emotions, stop, describe how you're feeling, and pray. "Lord, everything about this day is falling apart. I don't feel like You see me. I don't feel like You care. But Your Word says You see me. You set me aside for a purpose before I was ever born. I will cling to You and Your truth."

When Self-Care Feels Bad

"Can I encourage you to talk about it?" my husband asked me.

"No, thanks," I said quickly. I knew he was right. I hate it when he's right.

He continued working on his fence post. For a few minutes, neither of us said anything. He tried again.

"You and your dad were really close. You would benefit from processing this loss out loud. Would you please consider talking to someone? If not me, then a friend or counselor?"

I thought about my dad every day. I just didn't like *talking* about him. Avoiding the pain seemed easier. Talking about my grief sounded about as fun as peeling off a scab. What's the point? Plus, I was too busy to process grief. Taking the time to go into that goopy room in my heart would be logistically complex with five kids at home. Seeing a counselor felt almost indulgent.

"I'll consider it." That was the best I could do. No way would I actually see a grief counselor.

Months later, I was stuck. A foster child in our care was not responding to my best mothering efforts. My training and insight fell flat with this child. I hit a dead end and decided that I could use counseling to help me move forward.

Halfway into our session, my counselor asked me a question that stopped me in my tracks.

"Do you have any unresolved grief that you haven't fully processed?"

Excuse me? Where did that come from?

"I help clients with various issues, but my specialty is grief. It sounds like you have unresolved grief."

HOW DARE YOU POKE MY SCAB, I thought.

My brain searched for someone to blame—but who? Who pulled this bait and switch? I recalled the events that brought me here and it hit me. *It was You, God, wasn't it?*

Over the weeks, this woman drew out my grieving heart. In that small room, she helped me to see it in new ways, even transforming some of my pain into gratitude.

Sometimes when God calls us into His care, the road isn't smooth or easy. Often the steps to healing are wrought with uncomfortable heart work. That doesn't make the self-care any less important. In fact, the difficult work is often the best kind.

—*Molly DeFrank*

Faith Step: Is God calling you to care for yourself by facing deep pain you've been avoiding? Open your burden to a trusted person and process through your hurt instead of hiding it away.

I will praise the LORD, who counsels me; even at night my heart instructs me.

—PSALM 16:7 (NIV)

So much of life happens while we're sleeping. Digestion, bone growth, the creation of new cells. Science tells us as many as 330 billion cells are replaced every day, many during sleeping hours.

Our faith can grow overnight too.

A complex decision weighed heavy on me. Nothing life or death. But both the *yay* and the *nay* of the decision carried consequences, fallout. I'd prayed and considered the options. Sought counsel from wise people around me.

Worry once had a stronger hold on me. I'm still learning to set problems on an imaginary shelf at bedtime. It takes intentionality. But worry is a better insomnia inducer than it is a sleep aid.

Even in the night, God must have been speaking to my heart. I woke early, growing slowly conscious that a song of praise from Sunday's worship was still running through my head, and within the lyrics of the song lay my answer. I shouldn't have been surprised. Peace swept over me. I had laid my head on the pillow the night before with only one advantage—the confidence that God cared about the dilemma and about me. My being in deep sleep, close to unconsciousness, didn't prevent Him from counseling me.

If I'd been clutching worry to myself like a foul-smelling, moth-eaten teddy bear, would I have awakened with praise on my lips? Not likely. My role was to "shelve" the worry and allow myself to rest in God's faithfulness. And He answered.

—Cynthia Ruchti

Soul Rest

Some days, I can barely slog through. Exhausted by the hustle and bustle of life, burned out, I look for *anything* to bring sweet relief from the routine at the end of the day. Netflix or Instagram beckon me to mindlessly scroll through movies or posts, nibbling on my favorite (sugar-free) milk chocolate in one hand and a bag of chips in the other. What a joy to put my feet up and do *nothing*. Rest is my best friend in those moments. Don't I deserve to be distracted and oblivious to life? But it's all too easy to confuse an easy escape with true rest.

A constant refrain drips on social media: "You've earned this." "Why shouldn't you take a break?" "Jesus understands you're too tired for Bible study today." And other lies the world tries to shove in our faces. It's terrible advice, and it might satisfy a current need, but it will never provide true rejuvenation for our soul.

I'm a doer by nature. I plan my schedule, make my lists, and feel like an utter failure when everything isn't crossed off by the end of the week. But I know chaos and frustration can take over if I don't make time to rest. I tend to confuse rest with laziness, feeling guilty when I take time for myself. If I'm not doing or accomplishing, I'm wasting precious time. I forget that God *invites* me to rest and let go of my list: "For he who has entered His rest has himself also ceased from his works as God did from His. Let us therefore be diligent to enter that rest..." (Hebrews 4:10–11, NKJV).

I love to cook. Chopping veggies and making a yummy soup for my family gives me pleasure and a chance to take a break from writing, speaking, and serving at church. Going to the gym, watching a movie with friends, and taking a walk with my husband are some ways I rest from the daily grind.

Those are practical ways to rest, but the best rest is soul rest—the rest that feeds our souls. The best soul rest I know is spending time with Him. Reading the Word, listening to worship music, sitting still in His presence, and meditating on His goodness. It's up to me to do it.

—Kate Battistelli

Faith Step: What does soul rest look like to you? Make a list of activities that speak to your need to rest and connect with God. Intentionally schedule time for yourself to do at least one of those things, even if it's only once a week.

The Calming Effect of Water

I read a book called *Blue Mind: The Surprising Science That Shows How Being Near, In, On, or Under Water Can Make You Happier, Healthier, More Connected, and Better at What You Do* by marine biologist Dr. Wallace J. Nichols. He devoted most of his career to sea turtle research and then shifted his focus to study the connections between humans and water, especially blue water. He performed extensive research using self-reported results, brain scans, and other tests that showed time spent in, near, or even looking at water helps the body rest from stress.

This concept resonated with me because many of the most calming, peace-inducing activities I do are associated with water. Scuba diving, for example. I immerse myself in the ocean and listen to my own breathing while observing the underwater sights and sounds, and it never fails to instill a calmness in me.

Living in landlocked Colorado, I'm not often at an ocean, so I regularly take bubble baths, which have a similar effect of washing away the cares of my day. I also enjoy submerging myself in lakes, pools, streams, and especially hot tubs. I never knew why I felt peaceful when I immersed myself in water, but this book provided insights. Combining cutting-edge neuroscience with compelling personal stories from athletes, scientists, veterans, and artists, Nichols shows how water increases peace and diminishes anxiety. Just being near water or looking at large bodies of water, such as oceans or lakes, increases levels of certain "feel-good" hormones and decreases the stress-related hormones. Even the color blue itself is known to be a calming color. Psychology and marketing research shows that people associate the color blue with concepts like openness, strength, trust, and wisdom.

I'm fascinated when science aligns with my faith. I think God made us to physically experience peace when we are immersed in calm water. Psalm 23:2 (NKJV) says, "He makes me to lie down in green pastures; He leads me beside the still waters." Still waters—a beautiful image of peace.

I've made it a regular habit to immerse myself in water whenever the opportunity arises, and I will continue to make this a part of my "blueprint" for living a healthy life.

—Jeannie Blackmer

FAITH STEP: Submerge yourself in a warm bubble bath or a hot shower before bed tonight and see if this helps you relax.

White Space

"Use all the space on the paper."

I remember the admonition from my fourth-grade art teacher so clearly as she stood in front of the class, holding the large piece of paper in one hand, a Sharpie in the other.

"You kids leave too much white space on the page. I want you to draw lines all the way to the edge. I don't want to see any more white spots. Every square inch of this paper should be filled with color."

As I sat at my scarred desk, legs swinging against its metal feet, I ran the squeaking marker across the large rectangle of paper. *No white, no white, no white…*

The effort it took to fill up that entire canvas of 11 by 13 inches was exhausting in my nine-year-old mind.

The teacher had made it clear. If I didn't use up every square inch of that page, my art wasn't acceptable. I had to fill it. Cram it with color, lines, paint, smudges.

And I've been doing it ever since.

Fill the calendar with more. More activity. More opportunity. Good things. Valuable things. Check off that ever-expanding list of accomplishments and then add more. After all, we only have one life to live, so we need to take that bottle of time and jam-pack it to the brim, right? No white space.

Somewhere along the way, I've realized I yearn for white space. I need quiet. I need solitude. More than that, I need Him. Not the church activities or projects or programs. Just Jesus.

Too many of us are living our lives and filling our schedules as we do our plates on Thanksgiving. We are gorging ourselves to the point of throwing up. We are choking, cramming every single bite we can manage and then wonder why we're miserable.

We've forgotten the exquisite beauty and peace of white space.

Graphic designers tell us white space is vital for several reasons. First, it helps our brains process relevant information. Second, it gives emphasis to the most important focal point of a design. In other words, the white space is what makes the picture what it is. It's what defines it and gives it beauty.

The idea is presence over productivity. Peace over chaos. White space over busyness.

Breathe. Find the white space. That's where you'll find His still, small voice.

—Tara Johnson

FAITH STEP: What are some simple ways you can create white space in your life?

*He gives strength to the
weary and increases
the power of the weak.*

—Isaiah 40:29 (NIV)

The muffled, mechanical sound of the garage door as it closed was like music to my ears. I smiled. My husband and children were off to work and school, and my much-anticipated day of productive solitude could begin at last. I'd planned the day weeks ago. Circled it on my calendar. Asked off work. Cleared my schedule. And now that it was here, my mind immediately began sifting through the list of tasks I had planned. At the top: make significant progress on an upcoming writing deadline.

I began as I often do, with my Bible and my journal. But that's when I noticed how cozy and comfortable my couch seemed to feel. And my eyelids—why were they suddenly so heavy? And how did this blanket and pillow appear so conveniently beside me?

I shook my head and began pleading with the Lord. He knew what a rare luxury it was for me to have a whole 6 hours of uninterrupted time ahead of me, and He also knew I couldn't afford to waste it. Saying yes to the deadline had been a huge leap of faith for me, but I knew that if He was calling me to the task, He would also provide the strength and power for me to complete it.

"OK, God," I prayed as I walked into my home office. "Here's where You take over."

—Emily E. Ryan

Staring Out the Window

A friend started a morning routine she's maintained for a couple of years. During some seasons of her life—times when life held more chaos and pain than intentionality and love—it wouldn't have been possible.

She wakes to freshly brewed coffee—her husband makes it as a gift to her—and goes about her morning routine as she sips her first cup of the day. Then she and her husband snuggle back under the covers, enjoying their coffee and talking through or praying about whatever's on their minds. When her husband eventually heads to the kitchen to start breakfast, my friend spends time alone in their cozy bedroom, journaling her thoughts.

It sounds ideal to me. My morning routine looks decidedly different. Because our 120-year-old farmhouse has bedrooms on the second floor up very steep and narrow steps, after a brief visit to the bathroom, I immediately dress for the day, make the bed, and accomplish everything I might possibly need to do up there before heading downstairs. That may include cleaning a closet, putting jewelry back where it belongs, dusting, vacuuming, or cleaning the toilet and sink. No lingering moments under a down comforter with bracing coffee, though I know it will be waiting downstairs. Then I descend the steps, check all the mousetraps for critters, and microwave the cold-brew coffee I made the day before while my husband takes care of his morning routines.

During breakfast, we share devotions together—a great start. By now, my coffee is genuinely "cold" brew, so I reheat it and stare out the kitchen window.

Yes. The staring part is an important God connection. Before I head into my home office, I stand for a while, coffee mug clutched to my chest, and peer out at the world beyond. The weather and wildlife. The vastness of the sky. The progress of the garden. Newborn calves or colts in the neighbor's pasture a quarter of a mile away. It's not a magazine-worthy view, but it's ours. Ever-changing. And ever-rooting. This is the part of my morning routine I treasure, the part where I step back and take time to linger with God in this space.

Here's where we're planted. Here is where we're growing and learning. My thoughts are allowed to wander but always return to the simplicity and beauty of following Jesus. No matter the details of our morning routine—my friend's, mine, yours—there is wonder embedded in the intentional focus on the God we love.

—Cynthia Ruchti

Faith Step: Describe your ideal morning routine. How far off is it from reality at your home? What is within your power to adjust? What's your equivalent of the quiet-your-heart practice of staring out the window?

Restoration and Healing

I spent 2 hours this morning planning my spring garden. I have a garden planner with a full-page grid. I drew small circles representing the new roses I will plant and larger circles depicting the lilacs I will post at the corners of my house. I can't wait! My mom used to spend hours in her garden while I was growing up. I used to think, *What in the world is she doing out there?* Now I know. She was restoring her soul.

Like my mom, I have found that putting my hands in the soil nourishes something deep within my spirit. I don't have an enormous backyard, but I have already incorporated four planting beds, two plum trees, two peach trees, and two ornamental pears. This summer we had cucumbers, tomatoes, squash, zucchini, peppers, snap peas, peaches, and plums. Welcome to Aughtmon Farms!

Everything about gardening restores my soul. The delicious fruit and veggies that we eat at our table bring me incredible joy. The cool morning air that greets me when I go out to prune my rosebushes calms my mind. The fragrance of the daphne and lavender fills the evening air as I weed. Even my epic fails, like trying to grow peaches-and-cream corn, make me laugh. What the catalogs had promised would be a sweet corn with white and yellow kernels ended up being all tassel and no corn.

My best life includes moments when I nurture my spirit. Caring for my soul and finding moments of calm help me breathe. My anxious thoughts fall away, and I feel connected to God. Whether it is watching a hummingbird sip nectar from a honeysuckle bush or seeing new blooms emerge on a flower I thought I lost to a cold snap, I see His handiwork. His design. His whimsy.

Seeing God's attention to detail with each delicate leaf and blooming bud reminds me of His loving-kindness toward me. He has taken great care to design me—body, mind, and spirit. I am His handiwork. And it seems only right that being near His creation would bring hope and healing to my heart. He restores my soul.

—Susanna Foth Aughtmon

Faith Step: Take a moment to soak up God's creation by going outside in your yard or visiting a park. Spend time thanking God for His amazing world and for the wonderful job He did creating you.

Small Getaways

My husband, Ron, was a dairy farmer for the first half of our marriage. When he was growing up, his family always made time to take a summer vacation because it was the only way to get a break from the daily task of milking cows. Following his family's example, we decided early on to make a yearly trip a priority for our growing family.

I always looked forward to our family vacations. We took affordable road trips to various destinations within the United States. The trips replenished me, offering a much-needed break from my daily routine.

Family vacations were sparser as our kids became teens and young adults. The trips we took were more likely to consist of carting our high school or college athletes around the Midwest or, later, visiting our out-of-town adult kids.

One summer, as our firstborn was moving to Mexico to serve as a missionary and our third child was leaving for college, I grieved the loss of togetherness that accompanied our changing family. Restless, I asked God what was wrong with me. Though I would soon be traveling to Mexico, I felt as if He was telling me I needed a vacation from all the growing pains my family and I were going through.

It was then I realized that our vacations hadn't just been a break but a true rest for the soul. Just as Ron had needed to get away from farm responsibilities, I needed to remove myself from the daily work as a mother that affected me physically, emotionally, and mentally. I needed to tend to my mama's heart.

I planned a few short day trips the week before my son's and daughter's moves. One day, I went to a county park and hiked. The next day, I browsed boutiques and storefronts I had rarely visited. Another day, I went to a botanical garden and ate at its quaint tearoom. The experiences mirrored the activities we used to do on vacation. Though I was by myself, it was just the break I needed.

The experience taught me it's OK to be gentle with yourself when experiencing change, loss, or grief. Respite doesn't have to be a long vacation; taking a shorter time for relaxing activities serves a similar purpose. An hour in your day doing something replenishing becomes like a mini getaway—one that may make all the difference.

—*Brenda L. Yoder*

Faith Step: Plan to do something simple to replenish your body, soul, or spirit—go for a walk, spend time on an activity you love, or invite a friend to join you in something that will refresh you both. ❧

*Therefore, behold, I will allure her,
will bring her into the wilderness,
and speak comfort to her.*

—Hosea 2:14 (NKJV)

After suffering a miscarriage and its resulting infertility, I was convinced God had abandoned me. I felt utterly isolated, forgotten, and lost, dwelling in a dry, arid land with endless sand and scorching heat—a desperate place of seeking and *not* finding.

But I learned a huge lesson: God dwells in the middle of the desert. He alone makes the desert bloom, makes the arid ground pools of water that allow life to thrive in this place. The desert is where He guarded His people for 40 years, teaching, rebuking, and loving.

In His wisdom, Father led me there. God spoke to Abraham, appeared to Moses, and comforted a distraught Hagar there. John the Baptist lived, baptized, and preached there. Jesus's wilderness testing happened there. It's only a matter of time before He'll draw us all.

We go to the empty, sand-filled place, the dryness of the desert matched only by the dryness in our souls. Our thirst compels us to search and seek the One who satisfies. The One who can bring life back to our soul.

And when He compels us to the dreary place and causes us to hunger and thirst in the barrenness, He will show us that He *is* there. When we thirst for Him in the desert, we'll discover streams of Living Water.

Don't fear your desert and don't try to avoid it. Just watch your desert bloom and grow…

…and you'll find He's been there all along.

—*Kate Battistelli*

Joy

Finding the Divine

Routine bombards us each day. We act by rote, not thinking or considering why we do what we do. Annoyed by the pile of chores, we grumble through our days.

Is it possible to find joy in the daily drudgery? Can I wash dishes/change diapers/shop/cook/clean and see it as more than an annoyance to be tolerated on my way to the bigger calling?

Am I content to live where I am, satisfied with the season I'm in? I question, complain, fret, and compare my life to the dreamed-up ideal I think I deserve. Some days, the grass looks so much greener elsewhere, and the daily tasks nearly overwhelm me with their gray sameness. I don't always trust the One whose sovereign grace placed me exactly where I am. Sometimes I forget to ask myself, *How can I take the lower place, serve with joy, give, pour out, and live my life for others rather than myself?*

Not everything that happens to us is about us, but many times, it's about those who are watching us. Others watch our lives and wonder how we can walk with joy despite our circumstances. And believe me, they are watching.

I work hard to be content with the life He's given me, and as I take His yoke upon my shoulders, I learn from Him. He is gentle and lowly of heart, and I'm slowly uncovering His will for me.

I'm asking Jesus to teach me how to:

Change a diaper the way He took a towel…

Serve a meal the way He broke bread…

Love the outcast like He touched a leper . . .

Live each day with the joy He promised in Nehemiah 8:10: "The joy of the LORD is your strength" (NKJV).

Jesus showed neither prejudice nor partiality. Kings and commoners were all the same to Him. He consciously took on tasks that His audience would have seen as beneath Him. His every word and encounter were imbued with the uncommon and saturated by the unexpected.

Through His example, He says two simple words: "Follow Me."

Follow Me and live an uncommon, unexpected, joy-filled life.

Let's honor Him through our actions each day—to make the common task holy and find the divine in each moment.

—*Kate Battistelli*

FAITH STEP: What are some everyday tasks that *you* can make holy?

The Joy of Dance

When I was a child, dance was a huge part of my life. I spent hours at the studio each week in ballet, tap, and jazz classes, and our family calendar revolved around *Nutcracker* rehearsals in the fall and recital rehearsals in the spring. I knew I'd never be a professional dancer, so I enjoyed every choreographed move I could while I was young. By the time I went to college, I had already allowed my dancing days to fade into memory.

A dozen or so years later, it was my sister who first suggested I incorporate dance back into my life. She had volunteered for our church's dance team, which led praise and worship during vacation Bible school (VBS), and she was loving it. By then I had four small children and hadn't even exercised, much less danced, in years, so I said no and volunteered to lead a small group instead.

But when the week of VBS arrived and I sat in the audience with the first graders while the dance team led praise and worship from the stage, something in me began to ache. I tried to suppress the urge I felt to move my body to the music, but it was no use. Next year, I promised myself, I would say yes to the VBS dance team.

By the end of my first rehearsal, I knew I'd found my place. I was worn out, sore, sweaty, and overwhelmed—but happier than I'd been in a long time. It wasn't just that I was dancing again. It was that I was dancing as a form of worship. And that, I discovered, was a level of joy I hadn't even known was possible.

Now I look forward to the beginning of rehearsals every year. From April to June, worship becomes a full-body experience. Most of the dancers on the team are middle-aged moms like me, and we have an unspoken agreement not to take ourselves too seriously. We're happy to let the younger, more coordinated generation have center stage while we dance the best we can on the back row. What we lack in technique, we make up for in enthusiasm.

—Emily E. Ryan

Faith Step: What brought you joy when you were a child? Sports? Art? Music? Board games? Think about how you can add that back into your life—and your worship—even if it's on a small scale. ✎

This Wonder-full Life

To a child, everything is wonder-filled: examining the details of an insect wing, finding a shimmering rock, spotting a shooting star. Sadly, our sense of wonder dulls as we become adults and face the daily grind. We stop seeing the world through the eyes of a child—at least I did until I started beekeeping.

The world of bees is astonishing. For example, my first hive lost their queen, which could have caused the colony to collapse. Knowing this, the worker bees selected a few eggs already in the hive, created queen cells, and fed those larvae special royal jelly until a new queen emerged. Then all was right in their world once again.

The miraculous details of bee ecology are so intricate and elaborate that it has not only awakened wonder in me but also rescued me from being stuck in the monotony of my ordinary rhythm of life. Keeping bees opened my eyes and encouraged me to take notice of my surroundings and see the other wonders around me.

The more I noticed, the more I became curious, not just about the miracles of nature but about my family and friends too. I started to ask questions about aspects of their lives that I had never thought about before: "What would your perfect day be like?" "What would you like to accomplish in the next 5 years?" or "What is your earliest memory?" Their answers revealed things I hadn't known about what they valued, the childhood experiences that impacted their lives, and their hopes and dreams.

Best of all, I've awakened to a sense that God is in even the most commonplace occurrences: Watching the sun rise and set. Looking at the flowers in our garden. Watching a child play in a mud puddle. Seeing a horse run freely in its pasture. Feeling the refreshing cold water of a swimming pool on an extremely hot day. I'm finding delight in ordinary moments as I live this wonder-full life, and I remain in awe of our wonder-full God who created it all.

—Jeannie Blackmer

FAITH STEP: Take a walk today and look for something you were fascinated by when you were a child, such as a butterfly or a roly-poly (pill bug). Can you experience joy in that moment?

This is the day that the Lord has made; let us rejoice and be glad in it.

—Psalm 118:24 (ESV)

We bought a house where the previous owners were amazing gardeners. One plant baffled me. It was a thick, stalky
green plant, and I couldn't figure out what it was. Because it
looked ugly, I kept cutting the stalks down. It kept growing
back. Finally, I gave up and let it grow. In July, beautiful pink
tropical flowers bloomed, the size of small dinner plates.
Turns out it was a hibiscus plant.

I never imagined hibiscus could thrive in Colorado. As
I delved deeper into this exotic flower with showy foliage, I
discovered two types of hibiscuses—a tropical variety and a
hardy variety. The hardy hibiscus tolerates harsh, cold winters.
I felt as if I'd won the lottery with this lovely flower blooming
in my garden.

Each flower on a hibiscus plant only blooms for one day.
Every morning I'd take a look at the new pink flowers and
rejoice in the beauty they brought to my life that day. I think
this is how God wants us to live too—day by day, rejoicing in
the gift of each new day and spreading gladness to those we
encounter.

—Jeannie Blackmer

Wigs and Lemonade

When life hands you lemons, make lemonade," or so the saying goes. Sometimes there's not a lemon to be found but a startling hairpiece instead. Let me explain.

Not long ago I ordered a pair of pants from an online store. I was supposed to appear on a television interview, and I thought the pants would be cute paired with a top I already owned. The company promised the product would arrive before my interview. You know what's coming. Interview day came. No pants.

No big deal, I thought. *I'll have plenty of opportunities to wear them in the future.*

Two days after my interview, I opened my mailbox to see a very small, very flat package. I frowned. This package was way too small to be my pants, but I hadn't ordered anything else.

Intrigued, I slid the package open to discover the company had sent me, not my pants, but a wig instead. *Say what?*

I wouldn't have even minded that so much if it had been the right color.

I couldn't help it. I burst into laughter. *Thanks, Father. I needed that laugh.*

Shipping that cheap wig piece back to the company would cost more than I initially paid for it, so I kept it. You know what? That little scrap of hair has brought our family and friends more laughter in the past few days than I imagined possible. Friends plopped it on their heads and posed for pictures. It adorned pets, and ended up being in a favorite series of photos on social media that drew comments and laughter from far and wide.

God loves laughter. He created it, after all. He loves joy. I believe Jesus had a good sense of humor. Have you ever been around someone who didn't? They can suck the air right out of a room with a single look. But the Bible says Jesus wasn't like that. People came to Him in droves. They wanted to be with Him, touch Him, talk with Him.

Gratitude and joy are linked. We can't be full of joy if we're constantly complaining, and a heart that is wallowing in self-pity is a heart that has stopped remembering what God has done for them in the past and what He has promised to do in the future. If we want joy, we should start by being thankful for good things, the unexpected, the intentional, and even the seemingly weird things that come our way.

—*Tara Johnson*

Faith Step: Create a "gratitude list" of the quirky, silly things God has brought into your life that have provided joy or laughter. ●

Finding Sense in the Spin Cycle

B ad news," the appliance repairman said, shaking his head and peering up at me from my disassembled dryer. "I can't find a way to fix this. You're going to have to replace it." Dirty laundry lined the hallway behind me.

"Replace?" I blurted. "It's only 3 years old!" And 2 days before Christmas to boot.

"This brand isn't the best. They often stop working for no clear reason. If it were me, with a family the size of yours, I'd buy an industrial dryer. They're about $1,500 but very reliable."

"Fifteen hundred dollars!" Gag me with a lint tray. I took a breath. "Thanks for trying. I'll get my checkbook."

I walked into the kitchen, ready to blow. My husband tried to cheer me up. "Babe, it's going to be fine!" he said.

"Fine? I have a load of wet clothes starting to mildew, dirty socks from six kids that could stun a skunk, *and* we need to shell out $1,500 2 days before Christmas." I slumped my head into my hands. The repairman's voice jolted me from my pity party.

"Ma'am? You're not going to believe this, but I put the machine back together, and it's working just fine." The gorgeous hum of a running dryer tickled my ears.

"What?" I perked up, running past the seventeen loads of dirty laundry to embrace my trusty old cube pal. "Babe, did you hear that?" I shouted to my husband. "The dryer's working!" I felt like George Bailey in *It's a Wonderful Life* celebrating his bleeding lip—a sign of life! Hooray!

I joyfully washed and dried six loads of laundry that day. I had never been so thrilled to scrub out grass stains.

What was the point of all that? I wondered about my dryer inexplicably stalling out, faking dead, and then coming back to life again.

Ding! It was like a light bulb had come on in time with the chiming dryer. I smiled, suddenly seeing all God revealed to me through a 3-day laundry sabbatical.

How easily I allowed a temporary trial to steal my joy. Convenience and ease are not the source of my joy. So why would I allow a failing machine to steal it?

The more we cultivate and pray for joy in our hearts, the more it works to buffer life's inevitable setbacks.

How quickly we forget that our joy comes from a generous God who has given us all we have. He wants us to share in His never-ending joy, strengthening and sustaining us when we run out. All we have to do is ask.

—Molly DeFrank

Faith Step: Is there a temporary setback in your life that seems to have stolen your joy? Ask God to fill your heart with His joy, which never runs out.

A cheerful heart is good medicine, but a crushed spirit dries up the bones.

—Proverbs 17:22 (NIV)

I recently heard this story at an event where I was speaking:

There was a little old lady who woke up one morning to realize she only had three hairs left on her head. She looked in the mirror and smiled. "Lord, I thank You because I can braid my hair today."

The next day, she woke up and only two hairs remained. She looked in the mirror and smiled. "Lord, I thank You because today I can part my hair."

The third morning, she awoke and looked in the mirror to see only one hair remaining. She smiled. "Lord, I thank You that I can put my hair in a ponytail today."

The fourth morning, she woke up, looked in the mirror, and, yes, you guessed it, had no hair left. She smiled and said, "Lord, I thank You. I don't have to fix my hair anymore!"

Praise is a choice. Joy is found in our perspective. So many times, we are so focused on what we can't have, on our limitations, we fail to see the opportunities God has placed in front of us. A merry heart is one that knows He is guiding, protecting, and redirecting for our good and His glory.

Joy isn't about having the perfect life but about learning how to dance in whatever situation we face.

—Tara Johnson

Chemo, a Shaved Head, and Knowing He Is Enough

Some trials break us to rebuild us stronger than before. God allows our lives to be a witness to His sustaining power and love during our most difficult ordeals. He teaches us an important and hard lesson to learn: He is enough. His joy *is* our strength.

"My hair is really starting to fall out now." That's what my dear friend Mitzi wrote on her Facebook wall. In fact, so much hair had fallen out because of her chemo treatments that her husband shaved her head yesterday. She's always had beautiful hair, and I'm certain she will again. Maybe different from before, but still beautiful.

I have no idea what she's going through. Losing my hair would traumatize me. For women, our hair doesn't define us, but it helps others to distinguish who we are. I'm ashamed to admit it, but overcoming my own vanity would be tiring. Mitzi says it's no big deal—it's just hair after all—and her cheerful approach convicts me to my core.

The lesson in this? Here's what she told me: "Jesus reminded me that all of us will go through trials. I don't like this one, and I never would have chosen it, but He assures me that His strength is sufficient. I can fully trust His grace is real and it is all I need to get through."

As the chemo drips, as her hair falls out in clumps, she asks her friends to pray that her thorn will be removed. But even if it isn't, she hears Him whisper deep in her spirit, "My grace is sufficient for you, for my power is made perfect in weakness" (2 Corinthians 12:9, NIV).

As life hits harder than she ever bargained for, she knows He alone holds her life in His hands. We are watching her as she lifts up His name, lets His joy be her strength, and makes Him bigger than her disease, her pain, or her hair.

She's stronger than I am. I would be wallowing in a great puddle of self-pity, but she isn't. She's enduring a huge life transformation with grace and a lot more courage than I'd have if I walked in her shoes.

Jesus flat-out told us we would face trials. She didn't volunteer to be in front, but she's leading the way and showing us all how to walk through fire.

We don't want to think about tough times. But no matter what comes, let's remember He won't ever leave or forsake us. Then we will walk through trials with as much joy and grace as my friend.

—*Kate Battistelli*

Faith Step: Have you been through trials in your life? Do you have loved ones who have? Revisit that time and remember the lessons learned throughout. In your next prayer time, lift up praise to God for carrying you through it. ❧

Snow Angels

This morning I woke up to 4 inches of snow. The world was blanketed in pure white loveliness. Untouched, it looked like a winter wonderland. Each twig and tree branch was encased in twinkling frost. God was showing off!

It wasn't long before I heard little voices and shouts of joy coming from outside our front door. Our three little neighbors across the street were discovering the joy of playing in the snow. All three boys had small shovels and were working away with their mom, Heidi, to clear their driveway. And by working away, I mean adding snow back to the areas she had just cleared. I layered myself up with my boots, gloves, and puffy jacket and went out to do some shoveling of my own.

The snow was dry and fluffy. As I began to shovel strips of snow off my drive, my three-year-old neighbor ran over and plopped down in front of me. Splayed out in his snowsuit starfish-style, he proceeded to sweep his arms and legs up and down several times. As his mom called him back, he popped up and said, "There! I made you a snow angel!" I laughed and said, "Thank you so much! It looks great!"

All up and down our street, neighbors were clearing their driveways. Heads down, shoulders to the wind, they were getting the job done. But watching those three little boys play, chasing each other and shouting with glee, made me pause and think. *Where am I putting my head down and getting the job done, forgetting to recognize God is inviting me to find sheer joy in what He has accomplished?*

Even when I am experiencing a challenging parenting moment or a tight writing deadline, God wants me to find joy in Him. I can find pleasure in His creation, marvel at His greatness, soak up His peace, and revel in His creativity. If I don't allow myself to be distracted, I can find joy in the most unexpected places. It may be time to start making snow angels in the driveway a part of my winter routine.

—*Susanna Foth Aughtmon*

FAITH STEP: Do you find yourself focused on getting the job done instead of finding moments of joy in your life? What kind of snow angels could you incorporate into your daily routine? ❧

Getting By with a Little Help from Strangers

Traveling by air offers plenty of opportunity for frustration, aggravation, discomfort, and waiting in line. Like all travelers sometimes do, even with TSA PreCheck, I recently stood in a long, snaking, disgruntled line—but with a smile on my face. Years ago I discovered that even one or two joyful faces in a crowd can change the atmosphere. I wanted to be one of them. So I breathed deeply, practiced peace, and smiled.

A beautiful, stately woman in the snaking line a ways behind me possessed a loveliness that seemed as much from pure joy as from her complexion, hair, and eyes. She, too, smiled a lot.

When the line brought us within a couple feet of each other, she leaned over the barrier and said, "Excuse me. Do you mind if I ask about your shoes?"

Not a question usually directed my way. I'm on a constant search for shoes that will work for me. Startled, I stumbled over the words, "Not at all. I don't mind."

"What brand are they? I've been looking for something just like that."

Now, mind you, these were black, relatively flat shoes in an ankle-high, bootlike shape, made of soft material, with good arch support and a wide toe box. Someone else might get comments on their leopard-print stilettos or red-soled patent leathers that cost hundreds of dollars. But this woman must have had my heart—*I need comfortable shoes that feel like slippers and look presentable.*

I leaned on the handle of my carry-on bag and lifted my foot, bent my knee, and peered at the bottom for some sign of the brand.

The woman called out, "Oh, don't take them off! I just wondered."

As I held my foot aloft, the three women behind me who had been chatting up a friendship joy-storm came closer so they could read the brand for the woman with the regal look so she could find out what to punch into the online shopping app on her phone.

After our curious and brief exchange, joy carried me through the rest of the day. Strangers in a line of frustrated travelers, doing their best to help one another with something as simple as shoes.

Sometimes, living life joyfully truly does mean getting by with a little help from strangers.

—*Cynthia Ruchti*

Faith Step: If you've been on the lookout for something magnificent to boost your joy, try adjusting your perspective to find joy in "stranger" places.

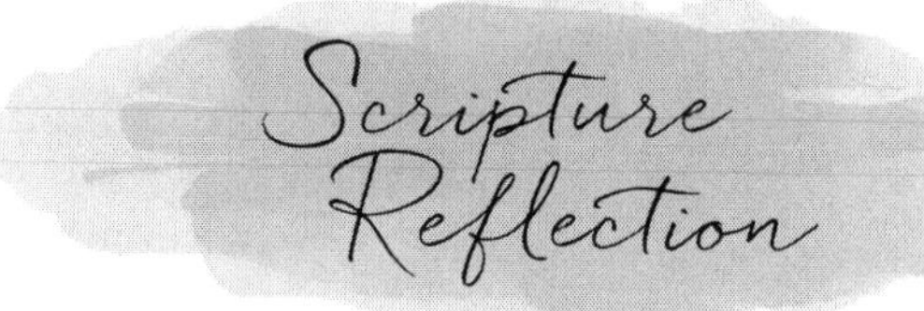

The LORD will take

delight in you.

—Isaiah 62:4 (NIV)

I talked with a counseling colleague about an internal childhood struggle with shame that sometimes arose out of nowhere. She leaned in and listened. She didn't judge me for the struggle. Instead, she assured me of God's love, saying He more than loved me—He delighted in me.

Delight was a concept I needed help grasping. The narrative of shame I've had since childhood was rooted somewhere deep in my bones. While I knew people in my life loved me, the outward demonstration of encouragement and joyful affirmation was muted. I longed for validation, and, when it fell short, I filled in the empty space with a narrative of rejection and shame.

My friend encouraged me to pursue God's delight. I began looking up Bible verses about delight, including a verse from Isaiah 62:4 that says God *delights* in each of us. I imagined some people I delight in—my grandchildren! I adore them differently than I do others. I show generous affection and excitement for who they are. Their mannerisms and individual personalities make me laugh and smile with love and joy.

Could God feel this way about me? I began envisioning and believing He did. I wrote down that portion of Isaiah 62:4 and taped it to my mirror to remind me of God's love for and joy in me. Shame slowly dissipated as I began to believe I was worthy of being cherished and appreciated for who I was.

—Brenda L. Yoder

Relentless Waves

I watched my son fight the continual onslaught of surf at South Padre Island.

The tide was harsh and the waves relentless as he attempted to slide onto a boogie board and swim into deeper water. Unfortunately, as determined as he was to leave the shallows, the ocean was just as determined to throw him back on the sand.

When a particularly hard wave sent his boogie board sliding from his fingers, Nate screamed with tears in his eyes, "I can't do this! Why does the ocean hate me?"

"There is a gravitational pull between the moon and the earth. It affects the tides," I said, keeping my voice soothing. "Those waves are just doing what God made them to do. I know you're frustrated. If you want to take a break, I'll rest with you. If you want to keep trying, I'll stay by your side."

He squared his shoulders. "I didn't know the moon changes the waves." Jutting out his chin, he headed back into the surf as I shadowed his steps. "I'm not gonna let the moon get me!"

In just a few moments, he had climbed atop the boogie board and was happily laughing with his siblings.

An hour later, I toweled off his wet hair.

"I'm very proud of you, buddy. You could have given up, but you kept trying."

Nate grinned. "It helped knowing what was making the water act that way. And I knew I would have fun once I got past the hard part."

Maybe that's one of the secrets to never giving up. Knowledge scatters mystery. The waves were just as powerful during Nate's second jaunt into the ocean, but he felt a sense of control in knowing the mechanics of tides.

Or perhaps it has more to do with faith. My son trusted that if he powered through the hard stuff, joy would be waiting. And it was.

When storms pound our backs, churning and spitting us onto sand, we can't give up. There is joy on the other side if we persevere. God gives His children exactly what we need to overcome.

Nate never knew it was my hand under the board, steadying it in the shifting water, that finally allowed him to climb on and ride the waves. We can do nothing from our own strength. It comes from the One who is with us in the tumult.

—*Tara Johnson*

FAITH STEP: Make a list of things you can do to strengthen your faith when facing a personal storm. Many of us will do things like pray more, read the Bible, or seek comfort from friends, but don't discount powerful tools like getting enough sleep, eating well, or practicing gratitude. ✎

Chopped at Home

For my son Jordan's thirtieth birthday dinner, I wanted to do something unusual to create a good memory for all of us. I had heard about planning an at-home cooking competition based on the popular TV show *Chopped*. In this program, chefs face off against each other, making a three-course meal in three rounds using different surprise ingredients for each course. At the end of each round, judges select which chefs are "chopped" until one is left as the winner. Because my boys, their significant others, and my husband, Zane, are all competitive, it sounded like something they'd enjoy.

For our family at-home version, I decided each team would make an appetizer. We had three teams of two people, leaving me to judge their creations. I purchased four ingredients for each team—packaged wild yellowfin tuna, cream cheese, a zucchini, and a mango—and put them into a bowl to be revealed at the beginning of the competition. Each team had 30 minutes (based on the number of years of Jordan's life) to create, plate, name, and describe their creation. They had to use each ingredient but could also get anything they wanted out of our fridge, spice rack, or pantry.

After lots of laughing, a few competitive verbal jabs, four bewildered dogs scouring the floor for dropped treats, and the "chefs" causing mayhem in the kitchen, we ended up with some tasty appetizers. The winners were Jordan, who's an amazing cook, and his wife, Laura Lee. They crafted a delicious roasted jalapeño pepper stuffed with tuna, chopped Italian salami, zucchini, parmesan, and cream cheese, topped with a reduction sauce containing balsamic vinegar, mango, and chili pepper. It was impressive! The prize? A handy and compact food chopper.

Experiencing a joy-filled family activity is good for everyone's souls. Our family times haven't always been fun and games. We've endured significant challenges, including health issues, addiction, job loss, heartbreak, and a wildfire destroying our home. Creating intentional time to play together helps build positive memories to last a lifetime and brings us closer, giving us strength to withstand life's trials better together.

—*Jeannie Blackmer*

FAITH STEP: Try your own version of *Chopped* at home with family or friends. You can find all you need for every age with a Google search for ideas. Don't forget the prize!

Unlocking Joy through Remembering

Our home is surrounded by lush, rolling grassy hills. Verdant filled with bunnies frolicking, birds chirping, life flourishing. When we first visited our home with the real estate agent, the first thing I noticed was 360 degrees of bright grass stretching as far as the eye could see. Well, in the spring anyway.

By the time May creeps into June, the sun hangs higher and hotter, and it lingers a little longer. Those rays singe the green hills yellow. I've learned to savor those last weeks of green. Life evaporating. You can watch the change in real time, if you're paying attention.

One gloomy December afternoon, the hills looked particularly grim. Soggy black grass and dirt matted the hills. They were so dark, I almost forgot that a few months ago they had brimmed with life.

"Remember when those hills were green?" I pointed to the black-gray mix of mud and dead brush. "Look how dreary, how *dead* the hills are! I know that they'll get green again in the spring. But it's been so long that my mind is having trouble remembering them that way."

"I know what you mean, Mom!" my little Caroline said. "When will the green come back?"

Not 2 weeks later, we noticed it—tiny flecks of green interspersed in the dormant hills. New life.

The hills reminded me of the power of this truth: new life will always bloom in spring. But spring wouldn't sprout anything if it weren't for the wet winter before it.

I can apply the same exercise to the dark seasons of my heart.

When I remember that life and new hope will indeed come, it keeps me from despairing in a season of matted, dark, and lifeless moments.

The loss of a loved one, a difficult work season, a strained relationship. When the landscape before me looks like a murky wasteland, I must work to remember that this is a season, not a permanent condition.

My joy does not need to depend on what my eyes can see. If it did, I would be tossed around like a rowboat in a hurricane. Calling truth to mind is like sending an anchor down, nestling our hearts into the deep, thick soil of joy that doesn't shift or change.

I choose to cling to the memory and promise that a new season is coming. That choice carries my heart through the deep, murky waters, planting my heart in solid ground.

—*Molly DeFrank*

FAITH STEP: Call to mind a season of joy and new life in your faith walk. Remember a season of slow growth or stagnation. Did either season last forever? Pray for faith to trust God no matter the season.

You have made known to me the ways of life; You will make me full of joy in Your presence.

—Acts 2:28 (NKJV)

My newest grandbaby was born a little before midnight. My son and daughter-in-law valued those early hours alone with their newborn. Long labor prior to an eventual C-section meant everyone involved, including my son, needed to heal from the adventure.

So I waited as patiently as a grammie can. I knew this precious little boy was "here" in a hospital 15 miles north of us, doing well. I knew the stats of his height, weight, and not-unexpected cone head. I'd even seen an image captured by an overjoyed daddy.

But I longed for the moment I could be in the child's presence. Hold him. Sing "Jesus Loves Me" in his ear as I have with every newborn in our family. Feel that unexplainably satisfying weight of a swaddled, scrunched-up infant in my arms and against my heart.

The joy of our grandson's birth carried me through the waiting. But it was a partial joy. I knew *of* him. I had yet to be *near* him.

The message came through late in the afternoon. Bumpa and Grammie could visit the expanded little family. A 20-minute car drive into town later, the two of us were welcomed into the hospital room and handed Grandchild #7. In that moment, I understood a little more deeply the concept of fullness of joy.

We can know of God. Memorize His attributes. Love Him. But knowing and nearness are two different things. In God's presence—proximity, closeness, developing intimacy—is *fullness* of joy.

—Cynthia Ruchti

Chasing Love

My niece Lily is 7 years old. She has one of the best laughs you have ever heard. But those laughs are hard-won. Our families lived close to each other until 4 years ago, and now we rarely see each other. When my family goes to Colorado to visit each Christmas, there is usually a warming-up period before Lily will bestow a gracious smile upon her cousins.

This last week, my sons Will and Addison got to spend time with Lily at my mom and dad's house. She tried her best to ignore them, but they persisted. They wanted in on bringing Lily joy.

Addie is 10 years older than Lily. He kept asking her, "Hey, how's my bestie doing?" Lily would scowl and say, "I'm not your bestie." He would grin and say, "I know you don't mean that, bestie." Her response would be an even louder, "I'm not your bestie!"

When this didn't work, Addie tried teasing her by saying, "You are my favorite cousin, Stacie!" "My name isn't Stacie. It's Lily." He laughed and said, "OK, Stacie." She showed a hint of a smile.

Will, who is 20, took a different approach. He chased Lily up and down the stairs, then around the ping-pong table and the kitchen table. As she rounded the sofa in the living room, she turned, grinning, and put her palm out, "Will, stop!" Will stopped and said, "What?" "Stop chasing me!" "I'm not chasing you!" "You are chasing me!" At this point, they were both laughing. Mission accomplished.

There is something wonderful about being wanted, isn't there? Lily knew that her cousins loved her and wanted to spend time with her. They wouldn't give up until they had her attention. The result? Joy unleashed.

There are moments in my life when I can run from the One who loves me most of all. But even when I resist His gentle nudges or wander from His grace, He chases me with His love. He is persistent with His grace. He wraps me in His mercy. He won't give up until He has my attention. When I give in to the chase and return His deep love, it is joy unleashed. Mission accomplished.

—Susanna Foth Aughtmon

FAITH STEP: Write out Psalm 23:6 (MSG): "Your beauty and love chase after me every day of my life. I'm back home in the house of GOD for the rest of my life." Place it in your pocket and meditate on it throughout the day as a joyful reminder that God is chasing after you with His love. ●

Serving Joyfully

I have worked with children and youth for most of my adult life, from the time I taught a junior-high Sunday school class while in college. I have mentored teens and have been a youth group leader, a public high school teacher, and a school counselor and therapist to teens and elementary students.

While doing all this, I've raised four kids whose activities and sports overtook our social calendar and volunteer commitments. I was grateful for the coaches, youth leaders, and mentors who poured into my kids during these years. They had the energy to keep pace with young children that I no longer did.

During these busy child-rearing years, my husband and I didn't do much outside our jobs and parenting. Now that our adult kids have moved away, our home and calendar are emptier. I'm not ready to be so busy again. I enjoy the quieter spaces and finally having some time of my own.

However, I was recently made aware of a need while serving on our church's elder board. Our small, rural congregation had not had a youth program for a few years because of the pandemic and a lack of high school–aged students attending church. The absence of a program for current teens bothered me because the youth group had been an important part of my children's faith experience. As a parent, I had valued the adults who led the group because I knew how important the ministry was to my kids.

As my time on the elder team ended, I suggested to my husband that we volunteer a couple of nights a month to restart and lead a youth group. The past youth groups met weekly. I was unsure if we were ready for that level of commitment. But twice a month—we could do that!

We presented the idea to the pastor and church leaders. They agreed a youth program was needed if we were willing to lead it. We said yes and proceeded to design a youth ministry that fit our energy and time commitment.

Being around teens has helped us adjust to our empty nest. We both enjoy and look forward to our time with them as we have fun and build meaningful relationships. Not only does this new endeavor meet a need for someone else's child, but it's also a bright spot in our life at this stage—bringing us the twin joys of serving others and spending time with wonderful kids.

—*Brenda L. Yoder*

FAITH STEP: Is there an interesting opportunity or invitation before you? Consider how stepping toward it and committing to it may enrich your life.

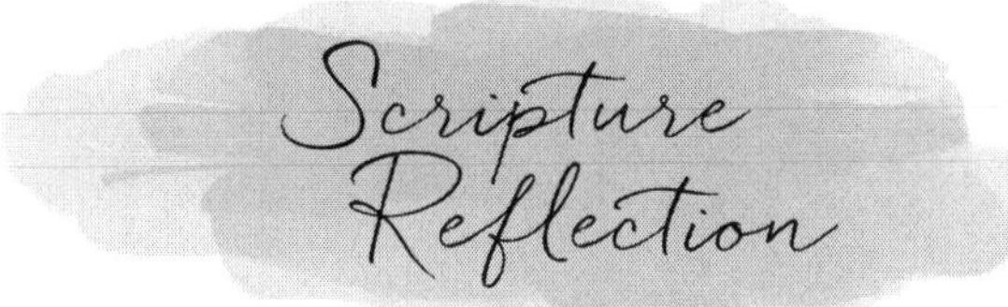

*Many, L*ORD*, are asking, "Who will bring us prosperity?" Let the light of your face shine on us. Fill my heart with joy when their grain and new wine abound.*

—PSALM 4:6–7 (NIV)

I always love hearing about how my friends and family are doing. But I will admit there can be small twinges of envy in my heart when they tell me about fun things they're doing, like amazing trips to Mexico. Or children going to college just minutes away from home. Or fantastic writing opportunities that I'm not a part of.

Why is that? I think it is because my heart is focused on me. I get distracted comparing my life with the lives of those I love. I start thinking maybe I am missing out on some joy I should be having. *Can I still live my best life when things aren't going the way that I want them to? Can I be fulfilled when there are struggles in my life? Or my career doesn't look like I want it to at this point?* Yes, I can!

But not if my eyes are fixed on others. I need to turn my face toward the Son. I need the light of God's face to shine on me. The truth is that joy doesn't come from my circumstances. It comes from soaking up His radiant love. No matter what is going on in my life, I can pray, "Let the light of Your face shine on me, Lord, and fill me with Your joy!"

—Susanna Foth Aughtmon

CHAPTER 6

Relationships

The Boy in 22F

I was sitting on a rumbling plane in Chicago, waiting for the painfully slow pilot to push us back from the gate. No one seemed to be in a hurry that morning. Even the ground controllers outside my window appeared to be dragging their feet. I blinked the grit from my eyes. The stale air blowing through the circular vents overhead wasn't helping. Everyone seemed sluggish…except for the four-year-old boy seated behind me in 22F.

The squirming tyke was chattering nonstop in his high-pitched voice, barely stopping for breath, peppering his dad with question after question.

"Why are these seats so big?"

"Will we get ice cream on this plane?"

"Will we be flying into outer space?"

I found myself smiling at his contagious enthusiasm. I set down the book I was trying to read as God impressed this directive into my heart: *listen.*

The boy had apparently pressed his face up against the window, for his voice sounded muffled. "Why are those men waving their arms?"

His father patiently replied, "They signal the pilot and other workers where to go."

The boy grew silent for a moment when a vehicle must have caught his eye. "What about that one, Daddy? What is that truck for?"

"I'm sorry, buddy. I have no idea." The father leaned in. "I wish I could tell you the answer. Are you upset I don't know?"

The boy giggled. "Don't be silly. I don't need all the answers. I just like having fun with you!"

And then I knew why God had me eavesdrop on their conversation. The boy in 22F was teaching me, and anyone else who was willing to listen, a beautiful lesson.

The most important relationship we can ever have is the one with our Creator. Speaking for myself, I often come to God with my questions and frustrations. That is certainly not wrong, but sometimes I'm more focused on gaining answers than I am sitting in His presence. There is tremendous joy in just being with Him. Our relationship isn't dependent on answers because my trust isn't based on what He *does* but is grounded on who He *is*.

I want a relationship with my Father that reflects the way the little boy in 22F looked up to his. *No answers needed.*

—Tara Johnson

FAITH STEP: Spend some time in prayer today thanking God for who He is. Reaffirm your love to Him.

Correct in Private

My family and I celebrated the beginning of summer by going to a local Mexican restaurant together. The small family-owned location is always busy, but they seated our party of six quickly, and my children were happy they brought two sets of chips and salsa to our table. I was happy to have another school year behind us and the entire summer before us.

We noticed the family across the aisle just after the waiter took our orders. A mother and her teenage daughter had finished their meals, and the mom had raised her voice just loud enough that we glanced briefly in their direction before returning to planning our summer bucket lists. Before long, the mother's voice was so loud it was drawing the attention of patrons several tables over. She was berating her daughter, and it became impossible not to overhear the details of their disagreement. It had something to do with the girl's stepfather, his generosity, Taylor Swift tickets, and the word *ungrateful*. We could fill in the details pretty easily. But just when it seemed the mom had made her point, she kept going, so much that we lost count of the number of times she said, "You have no respect for me!" while the girl sat in silence, staring down at her half-eaten plate of enchiladas.

On the way home, we talked about how awkward and inappropriate the public squabble was. "No wonder the daughter didn't respect her mom," my son said. "I wouldn't respect you either if you yelled at me in public like that."

His comment reminded me of a lesson I had recently heard from Matthew 18:15–17. In those verses, Jesus teaches that a person's sins should first be discussed privately between the person who was at fault and the person who learned about it. It's a guideline designed to bring restoration rather than ridicule, and it's a practical strategy that can still be applied to all types of relationships today, whether it's between church members, coworkers, or family members.

Seeing the results of a public confrontation that day, my family agreed that we'd all prefer to be treated with the kind of respect Jesus describes. We made a family vow to speak positively about each other in public and keep our difficult conversations private.

—Emily E. Ryan

Faith Step: The next time you need to address an issue with a friend or family member, follow Jesus's command in Matthew 18:15 and address the sin privately. Or, as the saying goes, "Praise in public. Correct in private."

The Hard Relationships

I was having a hard time with an extended family member. Really hard. I finally talked with a counselor about how to navigate the relationship, mainly because banging my head against a wall wasn't getting me anywhere.

I worked myself into knots for years trying to make this relationship successful, waiting for a breakthrough that never came. *Maybe it'll be different this time. Maybe something will click for her, and we can move on together in harmony.* But I knew better than to expect the conflict to evaporate overnight.

I knew that relationships were difficult for her. I knew that communication was a challenge. I knew that staying composed during conflict was not her strong suit. I knew that even if I forgave the mean things she often said, I would have trouble forgetting.

And I knew that I was called to love her through it.

Still, I couldn't shake the nagging allure of an easier, simpler, more enjoyable life—a life where relating to this person was no longer required. What if I just…checked out?

"Have you noticed," the therapist asked me, "that God is not like us? While we move away from people who wrong us, from difficulty, He moves *toward* us?"

She was right.

God is not repelled by the parts of us that are hard to love. He is never annoyed to the point of walking away from us.

And yet, I sure am.

In all relationships, of course, appropriate boundaries are needed. But in this one, I knew that the right thing was for me to reflect the kind of love that God shows me.

"How am I going to do this?" I asked her. "I'm at the end of myself. I need more compassion, forgiveness, lovingkindness. But I am all out."

"Yes." She smiled. "You need strength outside of yourself."

We learn to see our own spiritual poverty through relationships with difficult people. Through hard relationships, we learn about the limitless love and provision of God. We more humbly see our faults. Best of all, we clearly see the places our hearts will grow as we learn to enjoy and even to love people we didn't think possible.

Another beautiful freedom we can learn: We are not beholden to our feelings. We can pursue higher purposes like love, peace, and patience. We can move toward people who are hard to love—even when we don't *feel* like it.

—*Molly DeFrank*

Faith Step: Think of a difficult relationship in your life. How can you see God's hand at work? Pray for what you need to navigate through it: Patience? Grace? Love? Endurance? Forgiveness?

The LORD gave and the LORD
has taken away; may the name
of the LORD be praised.

—JOB 1:21 (NIV)

Despite my best efforts to repair a strained relationship, I couldn't change Melanie's perception of the hurt I caused her years ago. I went to work and forced a smile as I interacted with others, trying to hide my unhappiness over the situation even as anxiety tightened my chest.

I wanted to talk through the problem with Melanie, but she told me that she needed more time. What if she chose not to reconcile? I didn't think I could handle the prolonged sadness of losing her as a friend. How could I carry on with my daily activities while waiting? I looked to the Bible for help.

I read about Job's multiple losses—first his herds, then his servants, and then his own children. In Job 1:21, when messenger after messenger arrives to give him more bad news, he responds in a way that might be surprising to some: He falls down in worship. He says that God may give or take away, but in either case, he would continue to praise God.

That perspective gave me hope. Happiness doesn't mean everything in life will turn out the way I desire. God allows sadness and loss amid the blessings in life. In praising God and focusing on His goodness, I could be OK despite not knowing if forgiveness would be extended or if I would lose a meaningful relationship.

Focusing on this realization lessened my anxiety and gave me the patience to wait for Melanie to work through her feelings. After several months, our relationship was restored. In the process, I had learned that peace isn't dependent upon getting the outcome we want—it's the result of God's constant care, through good news and bad.

—Brenda L. Yoder

How Strangers Become Friends

We moved to Nashville several years ago, and we didn't know a soul except our daughter and her family. We were in a new community, attending a new church, and trying our best to seek new relationships.

It was more difficult than I thought. I waited for others to reach out to *me*, not realizing it was my responsibility to reach out to *them*, to let them into my home and heart. Once I realized my mistake, I was determined to reach out and create community, using hospitality as the vehicle.

Once we had settled into our new church, my husband and I answered the call to start a home group. Every week, we started at 6:30 p.m., sharing food, fellowship, prayer, and a Bible study. After a while, some of our members asked if they could bring a friend along. Who were we to say no?

Jesus said, "I stand at the door and knock. If anyone hears My voice and opens the door, I will come in to him and dine with him, and he with Me" (Revelation 3:20, NKJV). What a beautiful challenge! He wants intimate fellowship with us and beautifully models how to extend it to others, lovingly embracing strangers and giving them a place to safely grow.

As our group has blossomed, we have watched it become a beautiful community.

My husband and I have received the biggest gift of all. Watching our home group grow, we've seen strangers become friends, and we have enjoyed the privilege of providing a safe place for many singles to fellowship and meet other singles.

We've had the joy of welcoming new friends, serving our expanding circle, and setting an example of inviting Christ into our home.

When I was growing up, entertaining was the byword. My mother did it very well, providing a beautiful meal with linen napkins, fine china, and lit candles. As lovely and pleasant as it was, I've learned hospitality and entertainment are not the same thing. One tries to impress, and the other is come-as-you-are, where you're welcomed regardless of your status. Our group isn't fancy. I don't have the perfect home, and I don't make a gourmet meal every week. Although I do love to cook, ours is a potluck, with me filling in the blanks.

Opening our home has become a way of life, a way to love strangers and see them become friends, and a way to model Jesus's love and welcome to all.

—Kate Battistelli

FAITH STEP: How can you begin to open *your* heart and life, turning the strangers you meet into friends and leading them closer to Him? ❧

Sacrificial Love

My husband, Zane, was diagnosed with severe acid reflux. Not only was it uncomfortable, but also the symptoms impacted his ability to sing while he played the guitar, something he loved to do. Even worse, his physician told us that if not addressed, the reflux could lead to esophageal cancer. So, we made some big changes to our eating and sleeping habits.

One major change was to our sleeping arrangements. Zane needed to sleep on an incline, so at first we put cinder blocks under the legs of the head of our bed. As a side sleeper, I found this was uncomfortable, so we ended up investing in a mattress that splits down the middle, allowing us to adjust our own side of the bed to meet our different personal preferences and needs. We also started eating dinner much earlier in the day, so he wasn't digesting food close to bedtime, and changed our eating habits to avoid spicy cuisine, tomato-based pasta sauces, and chocolate.

I didn't have the best attitude about these changes. The split bed reminded me of a hospital bed, and not eating foods I enjoyed became tiresome. It was also inconvenient to try to eat dinner every day at 4:30 p.m. I felt embarrassed telling our friends we needed to eat so early. Yet, I kept remembering the biblical principle of putting others' needs ahead of my own. A long-term relationship will require times of sacrifice. This has become my time to practice sacrificial love so my husband can thrive.

As time went on, I saw improvement in Zane's symptoms and his attitude. He slept better, and with the pain in his throat lessened, he began playing his guitar and singing more. Witnessing Zane's progress and hearing him play and sing changed my attitude too. I no longer felt uncomfortable asking people to meet us early for a bite to eat. I mostly make low-acid foods when we're eating at home, and when I go out for dinner with a friend, I'll suggest a Mexican or Italian restaurant so that I can indulge in the foods Zane can't eat.

Putting Zane's needs above my own has strengthened our 37-year marriage. The minor inconveniences to me have been worth the results for Zane. He knows I'm here for him and in it with him, and I know he'd do the same for me.

—Jeannie Blackmer

Faith Step: What can you do today to show someone that you are putting their needs ahead of your own? ❧

*Like one who takes off a garment
on a cold day, or like vinegar
on soda, is one who sings songs
to a troubled heart.*

—PROVERBS 25:20 (NASB)

I was 3 weeks postpartum with baby number two. I teetered between sadness and despair, crying nonstop.

Postpartum depression was new to me, and I'd never met a more unwelcome visitor.

I sat in my mother-in-law's kitchen, crying. Looking down at my beautiful baby boy, I wondered how I could be feeling lower than I've ever felt while holding the most wonderful blessing.

"How are you doing?" she gently asked.

"I'm just sad all the time. I wake up, and I'm overwhelmed by the day before I'm even out of bed."

She looked up from the dishes she was washing. "I am so sorry you're going through this. It sounds awful. I can't imagine what that feels like." She shook her head, listening as I shared.

Much of that season remains a blur. But one thing that seared into my memory was my mother-in-law's genuine compassion for me. She didn't try to cheer me up. She didn't try to explain why I had no logical reason to be sad. She showed me the power of climbing into the pit with a person in pain.

How tempting it is to spew solutions to a troubled heart. But the downtrodden know that the best way to minister to a hurting person is to get into the miry pit with them. When a friend is willing to sit with us in our pain, the deepest ache inside our soul feels seen.

—Molly DeFrank

Love Letters

In the early days of our dating relationship, when we were in college, Scott and I wrote daily notes to each other. He was youth pastoring, and I was working at an after-school rec program. I had access to tons of art supplies: construction paper, crayons, markers, and watercolors. During art time, I wrote Scott love letters.

I penned my notes with great affection. He was so good to me that I wanted him to know everything that was going on in my life. I shared my hopes and fears with him. I told him how cute he was. (Nothing has changed!) When I met up with him at dinner in the cafeteria, we would exchange the notes we had written to each other. I hung on his every word.

Fast-forward 27 years, and we still have a plastic tub full of our love letters stowed away in our garage. Now text threads have taken the place of our notes. Scott sends me funny memes and keeps me posted about what's happening during his day. I let him in on my latest writing projects and fill him in on what our boys are up to while he's at work.

Sending a text or seven may not seem quite as romantic as watercolor painting a poster, but the spirit is the same. I love Scott. I want him to know everything that is going on in my life. And he wants me to know what is going on in his. One thing that hasn't changed over the last few decades of marriage is that if we want to stay connected, communication is vital.

I find that the same type of communication is needed with my Heavenly Father. Even though He is all-knowing, I truly believe He wants in on the goings-on of my life. He wants to hear about the ins and outs of my days, and He "bends down and listens," as it says in Psalm 116:2 (TLB). Our communication isn't one-sided. He shares His thoughts and truth through His Scripture and through those who love Him. He is so good to me. I hang on His every word.

—*Susanna Foth Aughtmon*

Faith Step: Write a love letter to God. Remind Him of all the ways that you think about Him and love Him. Tell Him your hopes and fears. Thank Him for who He is and all He has done for you.

Lion Sweaters, Life, and Lists

My family knows me so well. If it's not on my list, it won't get done. I have lists for *everything*. Weekly lists, shopping lists, daily lists, prayer lists, and more. Heaven help me if I leave my shopping list at home! Something crucial, likely what I wrote my list for in the first place, will inevitably be forgotten. I even write down the things I *know* I won't forget, like laundry and paying bills. I know I have to do them, but it's so satisfying to write them down.

And the payoff? Crossing it off my list. Done.

I finished knitting a sweater for my grandson recently. I'd planned it for Christmas and worked hard, but it was a challenging pattern—intarsia for you knitters. I kept making mistakes, ripping them out, and starting over. Missing my Christmas deadline, I was determined to finish it by Easter. But time got in the way, so I didn't.

Last week, I finished it. *Finally.* Every row, dropped stitch, mistake, and do-over was worth it to see my grandson's face light up when he saw it. I'd hoped and prayed it would fit, and it did.

What's the lesson in all this? I'm a goal-setter, a dreamer, and a list-maker. I see it all first. Some say, "I'll believe it when I see it." I say, "I'll see it when I believe it." Lists are one of the ways I see things—visualizing the steps toward where I want to be, giving myself a map to follow. Just like knitting, I need to see the final result in my mind before I start. But I know I won't get anywhere unless I follow the steps. Knitting takes time and can get boring, row after row the same. But each row connects with the next as you see it build and grow.

Suddenly, it takes shape and becomes real. Then you hit a wall and make mistakes you can't see right away, like dropping a stitch several rows back. Do you leave it or rip out those rows to fix it? That's when I remember 1 Corinthians 9:24 (NKJV): "Do you not know that those who run in a race all run, but one receives the prize? Run in such a way that you may obtain it."

Go back to the beginning and make it right. Keep working, embrace the challenge, endure the boredom, and run the race. Follow your lists—especially the ones that remind you to do the things that bring you closer to God. One day, you'll have something beautiful, something worth the challenge.

And best of all? You can cross it off your list! And see a new thing to believe.

—Kate Battistelli

FAITH STEP: What's on your to-do list today? Find the things that will bring you closer to God and focus on those first.

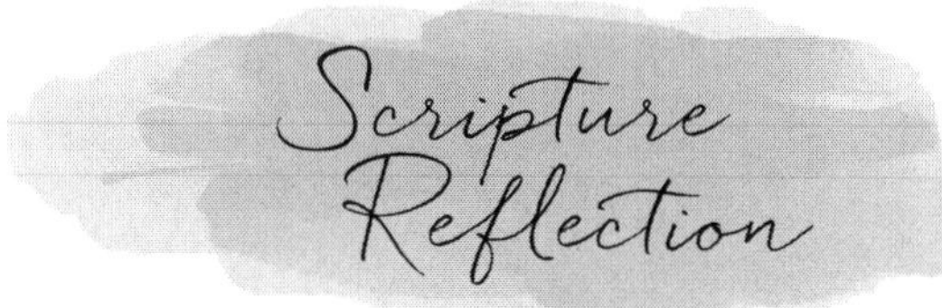

*[There is] a time to keep and
a time to throw away.*

—Ecclesiastes 3:6 (NIV)

I found boxes of trinkets from my childhood as we cleaned the attic above our garage. I'm notorious in our family for keeping things—I find it hard to let go of the tangible items that hold good memories and sentimental value. As I unwrapped items carefully put away years ago, some of them were easy to discard, but others left me conflicted. One of them was a brown plastic basset hound with sad eyes and a business logo around its neck. This sorry-looking dog carried fond memories of my dad.

My dad wasn't very demonstrative with affection when I was young. As the youngest of four girls, I often felt overlooked and overshadowed by my older siblings. Most clothes and toys I had were hand-me-downs. But one day, when my dad came home from a business trip with this little dog just for me, it made me feel special to him. It was hard to let go of the memory of that feeling.

As I debated, I asked myself, *Do I still need this little hound to make me feel unique or cherished?* God reminded me of the verse in Ecclesiastes that tells us there's a time to keep certain things and a time to throw them away. I realized that while the hound made me feel a father's love as a child, as an adult I have the daily love of my Heavenly Father and a caring community of family and friends. It was time to put the hound in the giveaway box. I did it with a smile.

—*Brenda L. Yoder*

Courage, Dear Heart

Every year, my sisters, sister-in-law, and I exchange "sister gifts" for Christmas. These small gifts can be anything from coffee gift cards to a package of fun snacks—just a little something to show each other that we care. This year, we weren't all able to be together, so I sent my sister gifts through the mail.

I had found the cutest leather and silver bracelets engraved with the words "Courage, dear heart." The words are from C. S. Lewis's novel *The Voyage of the Dawn Treader*.

In the story, Lucy—a girl from our world who has been pulled into the magical land of Narnia—is aboard a ship called the *Dawn Treader*. They are nearing the Island Where Dreams Come True. (Bad dreams, that is.) She knows she will be facing her greatest fears. An albatross circles overhead and whispers a message from Aslan, a talking lion that Lewis uses to represent Jesus: "Courage, dear heart." She is shored up by his encouragement and ready to face what lies ahead.

I don't know all the things that my sisters are facing. But I know that as we move through life, navigating work stress, ministry obligations, family growth, and our ever-changing culture, we could all do with an extra dose of courage. And we all need to be reminded that we are not alone. Strapping "Courage, dear heart" to our wrists just reminds us that we are held dear and that we have each other.

As soon as the bracelet arrived in the mail, I put it on. It reminds me of God's words to Joshua as he faced leading the

Israelites after Moses's death: "Have I not commanded you? Be strong and courageous. Do not be afraid; do not be discouraged, for the LORD your God will be with you wherever you go" (Joshua 1:9, NIV).

I tend to be anxious. I have been known to give in to fear on occasion. Facing the unknown can unleash negative emotions in my heart and mind. But then I remember that God is on my side. He is fighting for me and with me. He goes before me and behind me. He leads me, and He shores me up. And when I feel most alone, He is with me saying, "Courage, dear heart."

—*Susanna Foth Aughtmon*

FAITH STEP: Take a moment or two out of your day to notice your thoughts. Do you find that you are anxious or fearful? Meditate on Joshua 1:9 and remember that God will be with you wherever you go! •

Celebrate the Small Things

As an elementary school counselor, I love celebrating milestones of growth and success in my young students' lives. In my role, I support students with the emotional, behavioral, and social needs that impact their learning. Each day at work is different. Some days I teach classroom lessons, lead small groups, or support parents with resources and interventions. On other days, I help students calm down when their behaviors are out of control or they have emotions they cannot regulate.

Many days, there's not much to celebrate. Behavioral or academic growth in some kids is slow despite our best efforts and interventions. My colleagues and I can wonder if we are making a difference in kids' lives despite the hard work and love we pour into them.

That's when small, unexpected moments can seem like miracles. I was joyfully surprised one day when I saw second grader Mario laughing and smiling while playing in the gymnasium with other kids his age. Mario's explosive behaviors, dysregulated emotions, and poor attendance had negatively impacted his learning. He was behind in academic and social skills. We had worked with Mario and his mom for several years to implement multiple interventions at home and at school to build positive relationships, behaviors, and confidence. I longed for Mario to be a kid without so many obstacles.

Watching him play through the gymnasium window made me stop and linger. I watched him giggle and play with other students. What a change this scene was from last year! This school year, he was slowly making significant gains. Consistent attendance, a resourceful teacher, and other supports allowed Mario to catch up to his peers in many areas. I rarely needed to work with him as I had in the past. In that brief, carefree moment, I saw him living his best student life.

I stopped by my principal's office to share the scene I had just witnessed. We both talked about Mario's growth and mutually celebrated the hard work we had put into helping him over recent years, work that often seemed ineffectual.

The moment reminded me to celebrate the accomplishments of projects or people we pour into. Often in life we get so caught up in the work we're doing that we forget to celebrate the little victories. Finding the joy in these small moments reminds us of the Source of all joy and His constant, gentle support in our lives.

—*Brenda L. Yoder*

FAITH STEP: Write down one milestone that you have seen in your own life or the life of another. Consider any facet of growth, big or small. Then celebrate the accomplishment! ✢

*A new command I give you:
Love one another. As I have
loved you, so you must love one
another. By this everyone will
know that you are my disciples,
if you love one another.*

—John 13:34–35 (NIV)

I find it easy to love Jesus. He is for me. He is my friend. He advocates on my behalf before the God of the Universe. What is not to love? But I do have issues loving some of His kids. The ones who are disagreeable, opinionated, and rough around the edges. Or the ones who ignore me and make me feel small. Or the ones who disagree with me.

The thing is, Jesus isn't letting me off the hook. His Word challenges me to love the people He puts in my life, not because it is easy or rewarding, but because He loves me. The more I reread John 13:34–35, the more I realize that He is actually adamant about it. He doesn't say, "You can love my people if you feel like it, or if you all get along." He just says, "You must love one another." Because how I love the people around me reflects on Him.

When I step out of my comfort zone and love someone like Jesus loves me, it shifts things. It is a sacrificial, generous love. This is the kind of loving that can turn the world inside out and turn hearts to Christ. I think we should do it.

—Susanna Foth Aughtmon

ABOUT THE AUTHORS

Susanna Foth Aughtmon's writing career has spanned a decade and includes inspirational, devotional, and humorous books. She is a regular contributor to Guideposts' daily devotional *Mornings with Jesus* and has written collaboratively with musical artist Plumb, *New York Times* best-selling author Mark Batterson, and master storyteller Richard Foth. She loves to tell stories that connect us to each other and to the One who loves us most of all. The mother of three sons, she currently lives in Boise, Idaho, with her husband, Scott. You can connect with her at sfaughtmon.com.

Kate Battistelli is the author of the bestseller *The God Dare: Will You Choose to Believe the Impossible?* and *Growing Great Kids: Partner with God to Cultivate His Purpose in Your Child's Life.* She's a contributing writer to *The CSB (in)courage Devotional Bible* and the *SpiritLed Woman Bible,* and her writing has appeared in *The Joyful Life* magazine, *The Better Mom, MICI Magazine,* and more. She is one-third of the popular *Mom to Mom Podcast.* In addition, she is an honoree with She Leads Tennessee.

As a young actress in New York City, Kate had a life-changing experience, going from understudy to starring as Anna in the Broadway National Tour of *The King and I* opposite Yul Brynner for more than one thousand performances. Kate and her husband laid down their careers in the Broadway theater in answer to their first "God dare," moving out of New York City and into a life of homeschooling and home business. She lives in Franklin, Tennessee, near her daughter and seven grandchildren, and blogs about food and faith at katebattistelli.com. Kate serves women by encouraging them to step out of their comfort zones and into His irresistible future.

Jeannie Blackmer lives in Boulder, Colorado. Her most recent books include *Talking to Jesus: A Fresh Perspective on Prayer* and *MomSense: A Common-Sense Guide to Confident Mothering*. She's been a freelance writer for more than 30 years and has worked in the publishing industry with a variety of authors on more than twenty-five books. She's also written numerous articles for print and online magazines and blogs. She's passionate about using written words to encourage women in their relationships with Jesus. She loves chocolate (probably too much), scuba diving, beekeeping, a good inspirational story, her family, and being outside as much as possible. She and her husband, Zane, have three adult sons. Find out more about Jeannie on her website at jeannieblackmer.com.

Molly DeFrank is an author and blogger who helps families deepen their connection with each other and pursue a deep, abiding relationship with God. Molly writes about parenting, technology, and faith. She has been featured on many outlets, including *Fox and Friends* (Fox News), *The Doctors* (CBS), *Good Morning America*, *Mama Bear Apologetics*, *1000 Hours Outside*, Guideposts, MOPS, and more. She and her husband live in California with their six kids, three goats, two cats, and a golden retriever.

Tara Johnson is an author and speaker who loves to write stories that help people break free from the lies they believe about themselves. Tara's debut novel, *Engraved on the Heart* (Tyndale), earned a starred review from *Publishers Weekly* and was a finalist in the Carol and Christy awards. Tara has been published by Tyndale House, Annie's, and Guideposts. In addition to being published in a variety of digital and print magazines, she is a certified body language expert and has been interviewed on radio, television, and podcasts. She is a history nerd, especially when it comes to the Civil War, and adores making people laugh. She, her husband, and their children live in Arkansas.

Cynthia Ruchti's writing journey didn't start in the traditional way: "I always wanted to be an author." She worked in a medical chemistry lab when first married, then set that aside to become a stay-at-home mom. Amid gardening, sewing, quilting, throwing creative birthday parties, and eventually volunteering at her kids' schools, God brought a unique opportunity across her path—writing and producing a 15-minute scripted radio broadcast showing God's presence and faith at work in everyday life. The *Heartbeat of the Home* broadcast retired in 2012, and by that time Cynthia had published several books on her way to more. She and her husband live in the heart of Wisconsin, not far from their three children and seven grandchildren. Her life and her writing all fit under the umbrella, "I can't unravel. I'm hemmed in Hope."

   INSPIRED BY FAITH

Emily E. Ryan never imagined God's best for her life would include being a minister's wife, mother of four, writer, and junior-high English teacher. Yet, it's in this struggle to juggle that she gets to know the Lord more intimately. She writes about her goal to find rare quiet moments and claim them for Jesus in her latest book, *Guilt-Free Quiet Times*, which encourages women to ditch guilt and embrace grace in their devotional time with the Lord. A writer and speaker for more than 20 years, Emily loves sharing Jesus through her words and sees contributing to Guideposts' *Mornings with Jesus* for the past several years as one of the highlights of her ministry. Emily and her family live in the great state of Texas, but you can avoid the heat and humidity by visiting her online at emilyeryan.com.

Brenda L. Yoder is a licensed mental health counselor, school counselor, speaker, and author of *Uncomplicated: Simple Secrets for a Compelling Life.* Her other books include *Fledge: Launching Your Kids without Losing Your Mind* and *Balance, Busyness and Not Doing It All.* She has also been featured in *The Washington Post, Mornings with Jesus,* and the *Chicken Soup for the Soul* books. She hosts the *Life Beyond the Picket Fence* podcast and cohosts the *Midlife Mom* podcast and Midlife Mom Facebook community. Brenda specializes in faith, life, and family beyond the storybook image. She and her husband live on a farm in northern Indiana. They are parents to four adults and have two daughters-in-law and three adorable grandkids. You can connect with Brenda at brendayoder.com.

ACKNOWLEDGMENTS

Every attempt has been made to credit the sources of copyrighted material used in this book. If any such acknowledgment has been inadvertently omitted or miscredited, receipt of such information would be appreciated.

Scripture quotations marked (ESV) are taken from *The Holy Bible, English Standard Version*. Copyright © 2001 by Crossway Bibles, a division of Good News Publishers. Used by permission. All rights reserved.

Scripture quotations marked (MSG) are taken from *The Message*. Copyright © 1993, 2002, 2018 by Eugene H. Peterson.

Scripture quotations marked (NASB) are taken from the *New American Standard Bible*®. Copyright © 1960, 1971, 1977, 1995, 2020 by The Lockman Foundation. All rights reserved.

Scripture quotations marked (NIV) are taken from *The Holy Bible, New International Version*®, *NIV*®. Copyright © 1973, 1978, 1984, 2011 by Biblica, Inc. Used by permission. All rights reserved worldwide.

Scripture quotations marked (NKJV) are taken from the *New King James Version*®. Copyright © 1982 by Thomas Nelson. Used by permission. All rights reserved.

Scripture quotations marked (NLT) are taken from the *Holy Bible, New Living Translation*. Copyright © 1996, 2004, 2007, 2015 by Tyndale House Foundation. Used by permission of Tyndale House Publishers Inc., Carol Stream, Illinois. All rights reserved.

Scripture quotations marked (TLB) are taken from *The Living Bible*. Copyright © 1971 by Tyndale House Publishers, Inc., Carol Stream, Illinois. All rights reserved.

 Inspired by Faith

A NOTE FROM THE EDITORS

We hope you enjoyed *Inspired by Faith,* published by Guideposts. For more than 75 years, Guideposts, a nonprofit organization, has been driven by a vision of a world filled with hope. We aspire to be the voice of a trusted friend, a friend who makes you feel more hopeful and connected.

By making a purchase from Guideposts, you join our community in touching millions of lives, inspiring them to believe that all things are possible through faith, hope, and prayer. Your continued support allows us to provide uplifting resources to those in need. Whether through our communities, websites, apps, or publications, we inspire our audiences, bring them together, and comfort, uplift, entertain, and guide them. Visit us at guideposts.org to learn more.

We would love to hear from you. Write us at Guideposts, P.O. Box 5815, Harlan, Iowa 51593, or call us at (800) 932-2145. Did you love *Inspired by Faith*? Leave a review for this product on guideposts.org/shop. Your feedback helps others in our community find relevant products.

Find inspiration, find faith, find Guideposts.

Shop our best sellers and favorites at

guideposts.org/shop

Or scan the QR code to go directly to our Shop

Printed in the United States
by Baker & Taylor Publisher Services